Hunt's®
Good for You Cooking

INCLUDES EASY & TIMESAVING RECIPES

MEREDITH® BOOKS
DES MOINES, IOWA

GREETINGS FROM HUNT'S®

Can you eat an interesting variety of foods while you're on the run?

Is your family getting the correct amounts of the right nutrients?

Are you able to enjoy your favorite foods and still eat well?

With *Hunt's Good for You Cooking*, your answer to these questions can be a hearty "yes." Inside this book, you'll find more than 60 mouthwatering recipes that take full advantage of the Hunt's pantry of tomato products. What's more, each chapter helps you follow the smart eating guidelines set forth by the USDA Food Guide Pyramid.

The pyramid stacks up as an easy-to-follow strategy for meals that are chock-full of pleasure and variety. Begin with breads. Go on to rice and pasta, fruits and vegetables, then on up to dairy foods, meat, poultry, fish, and eggs. This book shows you how Hunt's sauces and tomato products team up with *all* the major food groups. You'll see how getting the recommended servings in block after block of the pyramid is a delicious endeavor, thanks to Hunt's.

So put your best foot forward and start climbing the pyramid. Your family will enjoy these healthy Hunt's recipes, packed with flavor and style. And you'll love cooking nutritiously-balanced meals from *Hunt's Good for You Cooking.*

TABLE OF CONTENTS

Pictured on the cover: Easy Pasta Primavera (see recipe, page 23)

Hunt's Marketing: Maureen Smith and Jeff Dryfhout
Hunt's Cookbook Project Manager, Technical Photography Advisor, and Test Kitchen Culinary Development Leader: Lena Mercurio-Cutler
Hunt's Test Kitchen Home Economists: Sharon Benson, Anita Dillon, Lisa Lukasik, and Rhonda Mayo
Editorial and Design: Meredith Integrated Marketing

HUNT'S®
PRIDE OF THE PANTRY!

Take the easy path through the food pyramid with Hunt's tomato products. Their robust tomato flavors, rich textures, and savory seasonings help you create fabulous meals in minutes. What's more, Hunt's tomato products are naturally low in fat, and many are available in No Salt Added versions. Set your sights on Hunt's for flavor and nutrition!

FRESHEN UP WITH HUNT'S CHOICE-CUT® DICED TOMATOES

Keep Hunt's Choice-Cut Diced Tomatoes on hand for use in recipes that call for fresh tomatoes. For this chunky product, the best choice vine-ripened California tomatoes are picked at the peak of the season to ensure maximum freshness and taste. Hunt's Choice-Cut tomatoes provide a quick-and-easy alternative to whole, fresh tomatoes in sauces, because the peeling and chopping are done for you. Stock up on every variety: plain or with Italian Style Herbs, Roasted Garlic, or Crushed Red Pepper.

TOMATOES: PLAIN AND SIMPLE

When you want really big pieces of tomato or prefer adding your own seasonings, start with Hunt's Whole Tomatoes, Stewed Tomatoes, or Crushed Tomatoes. These plump red tomatoes, the pride of California's crop, are perfect for soups, sauces, stews, and casseroles.

Use Whole or Crushed Tomatoes for a rich tomato taste, or try Hunt's Stewed Tomatoes with a blend of onions, sweet peppers, and celery. Choose from Original and No Salt Added versions.

YOUR SECRET TO SAUCE

Behind every good cook is a great sauce, and you can stock up on six—without any measuring, chopping or blending! Hunt's Ready Tomato Sauces live up to their name—they're ready when you are. These rich, thick sauces free your imagination to create family favorites in the blink of an eye. Four chunky and two smooth sauces boast all-natural ingredients and delicate seasonings ideal for meat, pasta, poultry, fish, and more.

THE STARTER

Talk about versatile! Hunt's Tomato Sauce complements all foods— from pasta dishes to vegetables, meats, and more. It's great for all types of cooking, too—from slow-simmering stews to shortcut entrées. Made from the highest-quality rich red tomatoes that are pureed for a thick tomato taste, this sauce is a shelf staple in any kitchen.

THICK AND HEARTY

Hunt's Tomato Paste thickens your favorite spaghetti or pizza sauce and adds zesty flavor and hearty texture to chili, soups, and stews. The tomato taste has just the right zip in all varieties—Original, Italian Style Herb, Garlic, and No Salt Added.

SCALING THE PYRAMID

It's easy to build well-balanced family meals using the USDA Food Guide Pyramid and Hunt's® tomato products as your partners every step of the way. Keep in mind that the pyramid is a tool designed for healthy people two years old and older.

THE PYRAMID PRINCIPLE

The pyramid is built from six food groups, each of which gives you most of the nutrients your body needs. To make your family's nutrition pyramid complete, choose foods from every group every day, and a variety of foods from within each group.

The pyramid suggests a range of daily servings recommended from each group. Just about everyone should eat at least the minimum number of servings, but the total number depends on the number of calories needed—and that is determined by age, gender, size, and level of daily activity. Each recipe in this book lists the number of servings it will make, giving you an idea of how large a serving should be.

The easiest way to think of the pyramid is in these terms: Eat more foods from the bigger parts of the pyramid and less from the smaller parts.

Keep calories and fat low by choosing low-fat options in each food group and going easy on fats and sugars at the tip of the pyramid. Hunt's makes it easy with flavorful products that transform the basic ingredients in each block of the pyramid into mouthwatering masterpieces your whole family will love.

USDA DIETARY GUIDELINES

- Eat a variety of foods.
- Balance the food you eat with physical activity to maintain or improve your weight.
- Choose a diet with plenty of grain products, vegetables, and fruits.
- Choose a diet low in fat, saturated fat, and cholesterol.
- Choose a diet moderate in sugars.
- Choose a diet moderate in salt and sodium.
- If you drink alcoholic beverages, do so in moderation.

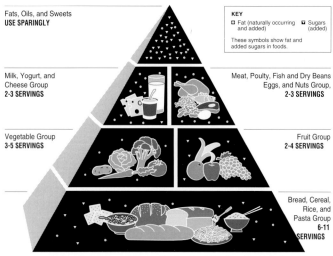

Fats, Oils, and Sweets
USE SPARINGLY

KEY
☐ Fat (naturally occurring and added)   ▮ Sugars (added)
These symbols show fat and added sugars in foods.

Milk, Yogurt, and Cheese Group
2-3 SERVINGS

Meat, Poulty, Fish and Dry Beans Eggs, and Nuts Group,
2-3 SERVINGS

Vegetable Group
3-5 SERVINGS

Fruit Group
2-4 SERVINGS

Bread, Cereal, Rice, and Pasta Group
6-11 SERVINGS

Source: U.S. Department of Agriculture/U.S. Department of Health and Human Services

THE PARTS OF THE PYRAMID

Each chapter in this book is devoted to one of the five major blocks of the pyramid. Throughout the book, you'll find recipes that show you how Hunt's products pair perfectly with foods from *each* group, resulting in meals that are simple and delicious. With foods like these, it's easy to follow the pyramid's guidelines. From the base of the food pyramid on up, you'll cook even better—and eat more balanced meals—thanks to Hunt's!

MORE PYRAMID POINTERS

- Remember—one recipe can cover several food groups. For instance, the Classic Southwest Casserole on page 54 contains tortillas, vegetables (tomatoes, corn, onions, and peppers), cheese, and black beans—that's four food groups!
- Stock up on fruits and vegetables. Easy strategies include keeping a bowl of fruit on hand for snacking, and piling plenty of Hunt's tomato sauces in your pantry to use in cooking—just ½ cup is equivalent to one serving in the fruit and vegetable group.
- Avoid adding extra fats and sugars, since they are found naturally in foods. Many recipes in this book help trim the fat by calling for lower-fat versions of ingredients.

BUILD ON

BREADS

There's good news at the base of the pyramid: Delicious and convenient, breads, pasta, and rice form the pyramid's foundation for healthful family eating. In this chapter, some of the world's best-loved breads— from pizza crust and tortillas to sandwich buns and a great homemade tomato bread—pair with Hunt's® tomato products for a winning variety of mealtime favorites.

Recommendation:
6 to 11 servings
from this and the pasta group

*Vegetarian Pizza
(see recipe, page 10)*

Vegetarian Pizza

1 tablespoon crushed fresh garlic
6 large fresh basil leaves, chopped
1/4 cup Wesson® Oil
   Wesson® No-Stick Cooking Spray
1 medium eggplant, sliced 1/4 inch thick
1 *each:* large zucchini and yellow summer
   squash, cut lengthwise into 1/4-inch slices
1 large onion, cut into 1/4-inch slices
2 medium red bell peppers, cored and cut in half
1 15-ounce can Hunt's® Ready Tomato Sauces
   Original Italian
1 12-inch prepared pizza shell
2/3 cup torn fresh basil leaves
2/3 cup shredded reduced-fat mozzarella cheese

In small bowl combine garlic and chopped basil with Wesson Oil; set aside. Spray *3* baking sheets with Wesson Cooking Spray. Arrange eggplant in single layer on *one* baking sheet; brush with garlic mixture. Arrange *remaining* vegetables in single layer on *remaining* baking sheets.

Broil *all* vegetables until skins of bell peppers are charred and other vegetables are roasted, turning as needed.

Reduce heat to 375°. Remove skins from bell peppers; cut peppers into strips. Set *all* vegetables aside.

Spread Hunt's Ready Sauce on pizza shell. Sprinkle *1/2 cup* torn basil leaves over sauce. Top with eggplant, zucchini, yellow squash, onion, peppers, and cheese. Bake 12 to 15 minutes; top with *remaining* torn basil leaves.

NUTRITION FACTS PER SERVING:
308 CAL., 10 G PRO., 38 G CARBO., 13 G TOTAL FAT (3 G SAT. FAT), 6 MG CHOL., 4 G FIBER, 588 MG SODIUM.
DAILY VALUE: 29% VIT. A, 86% VIT. C, 11% CALCIUM, 16% IRON.

GREEK TOWN PIZZA

MAKES 8 SERVINGS
PREPARATION TIME: 20 MINUTES • COOKING TIME: 25 MINUTES
STANDING TIME: 5 MINUTES

	Wesson® No-Stick Cooking Spray
1	16-ounce loaf frozen honey wheat bread dough, thawed
1	10-ounce package frozen chopped spinach, thawed
$3/4$	pound lean ground beef
1	cup chopped onion
1	teaspoon crushed fresh garlic
1	15-ounce can Hunt's® Ready Tomato Sauces Original or Chunky Italian
$1^1/2$	teaspoons chopped fresh oregano or $1/2$ teaspoon dried oregano, crushed
1	cup shredded reduced-fat Monterey Jack or mozzarella cheese
$1/2$	cup crumbled feta cheese

Spray 12-inch pizza pan with Wesson Cooking Spray. Press bread dough into pan, forming 1-inch edge. Using fork, prick dough several times. Bake in 375° oven 10 minutes.

Meanwhile, squeeze excess liquid from spinach. Sprinkle spinach over crust. In skillet cook ground beef, onion, and garlic until meat is brown; drain. Stir in Hunt's Ready Sauce and oregano. Spoon meat mixture over spinach. Sprinkle with cheeses. Bake in 375° oven 25 minutes or until crust is browned and filling is heated through. Let stand 5 minutes.

NUTRITION FACTS PER SERVING:
310 CAL., 21 G PRO., 35 G CARBO., 11 G TOTAL FAT (4 G SAT. FAT), 43 MG CHOL., 3 G FIBER, 732 MG SODIUM.
DAILY VALUE: 28% VIT. A, 13% VIT. C, 14% CALCIUM, 12% IRON.

SPRAY YOUR WAY TO MORE HEALTHFUL MEALS

Wesson® No-Stick Cooking Spray is a must for every health-conscious cook's pantry. Use it to spray baking pans, skillets, broiler racks, and grill racks instead of greasing them. (Always be sure to spray the pans or racks before you heat them.) Not only will you cook with fewer calories and less fat, you'll also make cleanup easier.

CROWD-SIZE CROCKERY BARBECUE SANDWICHES

MAKES 16 TO 18 SERVINGS
PREPARATION TIME: 30 MINUTES • COOKING TIME: 10½ HOURS

1	3-pound fresh beef brisket, trimmed
½	cup water
3	tablespoons vinegar
5	tablespoons Worcestershire sauce
1	teaspoon ground cumin or chili powder
1	28-ounce can Hunt's® Whole Tomatoes, cut up
1	cup chopped onion
1	6-ounce can Hunt's® Tomato Paste with Garlic
¼	cup vinegar
3	tablespoons brown sugar
1½	teaspoons crushed fresh garlic
¼	teaspoon bottled hot pepper sauce
16	to 18 Kaiser rolls or hamburger buns, split

If necessary, cut meat to fit into 3½- or 4-quart electric crockery cooker. Add water, the 3 tablespoons vinegar, *2 tablespoons* Worcestershire sauce, and cumin. Cover and cook on low-heat setting 10 to 12 hours or on high-heat setting 4 to 5 hours or until meat is tender.

Meanwhile, in saucepan combine *undrained* Hunt's Tomatoes, onion, Hunt's Tomato Paste, the ¼ cup vinegar, brown sugar, *remaining* Worcestershire sauce, garlic, and pepper sauce. Bring to boil; reduce heat. Simmer, covered, 15 minutes, stirring occasionally.*

Remove meat from cooker; discard liquid. Using 2 forks to pull through meat in opposite directions, shred meat and return it to cooker. Stir in sauce. Cover and cook on high-heat setting 30 to 45 minutes more or until heated through. Serve in Kaiser rolls.

*Note: Use the sauce immediately or cool it slightly, then transfer to a storage container. Cover and refrigerate up to 3 days.

NUTRITION FACTS PER SERVING:
352 CAL., 25 G PRO., 38 G CARBO., 11 G TOTAL FAT (3 G SAT. FAT), 59 MG CHOL., 1 G FIBER, 633 MG SODIUM.
DAILY VALUE: 7% VIT. A, 24% VIT. C, 6% CALCIUM, 28% IRON.

SPANISH-STYLE TURNOVERS

MAKES 4 SERVINGS
PREPARATION TIME: 50 MINUTES • COOKING TIME: 18 MINUTES

½	pound lean ground beef
½	cup *each:* finely chopped onion and green bell pepper
1	teaspoon crushed fresh garlic
1	8-ounce can Hunt's® Tomato Sauce
¼	cup raisins
2	tablespoons *each:* finely chopped pimiento-stuffed green olives and capers
½	teaspoon ground cinnamon
1	10-ounce package refrigerated pizza dough
	Skim milk
	Wesson® No-Stick Cooking Spray

In skillet cook ground beef, onion, green pepper, and garlic until meat is brown; drain. Stir in Hunt's Tomato Sauce, raisins, olives, capers, and cinnamon. Bring to boil; reduce heat. Simmer, covered, 10 minutes. Cool slightly.

Unroll pizza dough. On lightly floured surface, roll dough into 16x8-inch rectangle; cut into eight 4-inch squares.

Place ¼ cup filling slightly off center in each square; brush edges with milk. Fold dough over filling to form a triangle. Using fork, press edges to seal.

Spray baking sheet with Wesson Cooking Spray. Transfer turnovers to baking sheet. Lightly brush tops with milk; prick with fork. Bake in 375° oven 18 minutes or until golden.

NUTRITION FACTS PER SERVING:
319 CAL., 16 G PRO., 40 G CARBO., 11 G TOTAL FAT (3 G SAT. FAT), 36 MG CHOL., 3 G FIBER, 771 MG SODIUM.
DAILY VALUE: 6% VIT. A, 30% VIT. C, 2% CALCIUM, 24% IRON.

SAUCES ON THE DOUBLE

Keep a supply of Hunt's® Ready Sauces on hand to use whenever you need a quick sauce to serve with appetizers or main dishes, such as Spanish-Style Turnovers (see recipe above). Just heat the sauce in a saucepan and it's ready to serve. Hunt's® Ready Tomato Sauces Chunky Special or Chunky Garlic and Herb are delicious with the turnovers. And Hunt's® Ready Tomato Sauces Original Italian, Chunky Italian, and Chunky Chili are ideal as dipping sauces for chips, breadsticks, cooked shrimp, or veggies.

Mexican Stromboli

MAKES 8 SERVINGS
PREPARATION TIME: 35 MINUTES • COOKING TIME: 25 MINUTES

$1/2$ pound lean ground raw turkey or ground beef
$1/2$ cup chopped onion
  1 15-ounce can Hunt's® Ready Tomato Sauces
      Chunky Chili
  1 15-ounce can dark red kidney or pinto beans,
      rinsed and drained
$1/4$ teaspoon ground cumin
      Several dashes bottled hot pepper sauce
      Wesson® No-Stick Cooking Spray
  1 tablespoon yellow cornmeal
  2 10-ounce packages refrigerated pizza dough
$3/4$ cup shredded reduced-fat Monterey Jack cheese
      Skim milk

In skillet cook ground turkey and onion until turkey no longer is pink; drain. Stir in Hunt's Ready Sauce, *half* of the beans, the cumin, and pepper sauce. Mash remaining beans; stir into turkey mixture. Bring to boil; reduce heat. Simmer, uncovered, 5 minutes or until most of the liquid has evaporated. Cool 5 minutes.

Spray 15x10x1-inch baking pan with Wesson Cooking Spray. Sprinkle with *half* of the cornmeal; set aside. On lightly floured surface, roll one sheet of pizza dough into 12x10-inch rectangle. Cut into 10-inch square, reserving trimmings. Place dough on pan, allowing half of the dough to overlap edge. Spoon *half* of the cheese down center of dough on pan; spoon *half* of the turkey mixture over cheese. Brush edges with milk. Fold dough over filling to form a rectangle; pinch edges to seal. Repeat with remaining dough, cheese, and turkey mixture.

Brush tops with milk; prick with fork. If desired, cut trimmings into shapes. Place on tops; brush shapes with milk. Sprinkle with remaining cornmeal. Bake in 375° oven 25 to 30 minutes or until light brown.

NUTRITION FACTS PER SERVING:
279 CAL., 15 G PRO., 40 G CARBO., 7 G TOTAL FAT (2 G SAT. FAT), 18 MG CHOL., 4 G FIBER, 666 MG SODIUM.
DAILY VALUE: 2% VIT. A, 4% VIT. C, 10% CALCIUM, 18% IRON.

BRAIDED TOMATO BREAD

MAKES 2 LOAVES
PREPARATION TIME: 40 MINUTES • RISING TIME: 1¼ HOURS
COOKING TIME: 25 MINUTES

1	cup skim milk (heated to 105° to 115°F)
2	¼-ounce envelopes quick-rising dry yeast
1	teaspoon sugar
	Wesson® No-Stick Cooking Spray
1	14½-ounce can Hunt's® Choice-Cut™ Diced Tomatoes with Italian Style Herbs, undrained
¼	cup packed light brown sugar
3	tablespoons butter or margarine, softened
1	teaspoon salt
4	to 4½ cups all-purpose flour
2	cups whole wheat flour
1	tablespoon cornmeal
1	egg plus 1 tablespoon water, beaten
	Sesame seeds

In small bowl pour warm milk. Sprinkle in yeast and sugar; stir well. Let stand 5 to 8 minutes or until mixture becomes foamy. Spray large bowl with Wesson Cooking Spray; set aside.

Meanwhile, in bowl combine Hunt's Choice-Cut Tomatoes, brown sugar, butter, and salt. Stir in yeast mixture; mix well. On low speed, gradually add *2 cups* flour to tomato mixture; mix 30 seconds. Stop machine and scrape sides of bowl. On high speed, mix 3 minutes. Return to low speed and gradually add *1 cup* flour and *all* whole wheat flour; mix until well blended. If sticky, add more all-purpose flour, *¼ cup* at a time.

Knead dough in machine on low speed 4 to 6 minutes or turn dough onto lightly floured surface; knead by hand 7 to 10 minutes or until elastic and smooth.

Shape dough into ball. Place into greased bowl; turn dough over with oil side up. Cover with towels and let rise in warm place 1 hour or until dough doubles in size.

Spray *two* baking sheets with Wesson Cooking Spray. Sprinkle cornmeal down centers of baking sheets; set aside. Punch dough down; turn out onto lightly floured surface. Divide evenly into 6 balls; roll *each* into rope 12 to 14 inches long.

Line up 3 ropes, 1 inch apart on baking sheet. Starting in middle, braid by bringing left rope underneath center rope; lay it down. Then bring right rope under new center rope; lay it down. Braid loosely; repeat to end. On other end, braid by bringing outside rope alternating over center. Braid loosely to complete first loaf. Repeat braiding with *remaining* ropes to complete second loaf. Let rise 15 minutes.

Meanwhile, preheat oven to 375°. Gently brush with egg mixture and sprinkle with sesame seeds. Bake 25 to 30 minutes or until done. The last 10 minutes of baking, cover loosely with foil. Rotate breads once during baking. Cool on wire racks.

NUTRITION FACTS PER SLICE (BASED ON 32 SLICES):
103 CAL., 3 G PRO., 19 G CARBO., 2 G TOTAL FAT (1 G SAT. FAT), 10 MG CHOL., 2 G FIBER, 148 MG SODIUM.
DAILY VALUE: 2% VIT. A, 3% VIT. C, 1% CALCIUM, 7% IRON.

BREADS

Seafood Fajitas with Tomato Salsa

Makes 6 Servings
Total Time: 25 Minutes

1	14$\frac{1}{2}$-ounce can Hunt's® Choice-Cut™ Diced Tomatoes, undrained
2	shallots or green onions, chopped
$\frac{1}{4}$	cup *each:* chopped fresh cilantro and fresh lime juice
1	tablespoon vinegar
$\frac{1}{2}$	to 1 fresh serrano pepper, seeded and chopped (see tip, page 42)
$\frac{1}{2}$	teaspoon crushed fresh garlic
1	tablespoon Wesson® Vegetable Oil
2	cups julienne-cut red or yellow bell pepper and julienne-cut jicama
1$\frac{1}{4}$	cups julienne-cut zucchini
$\frac{3}{4}$	pound peeled cooked shrimp or shrimp-, lobster-, or crab-flavored chunk-style fish pieces
$\frac{1}{4}$	to $\frac{1}{2}$ teaspoon ground red pepper
6	8-inch flour tortillas, warmed
1	cup shredded reduced-fat Monterey Jack cheese
	Torn mixed greens (optional)

For salsa, in bowl combine Hunt's Choice-Cut Tomatoes, shallots, cilantro, *1 tablespoon* of the lime juice, the vinegar, serrano pepper, and garlic. Cover and refrigerate.

Meanwhile, in wok or skillet heat Wesson Oil over medium-high heat. Add bell pepper and jicama; stir-fry 2 minutes. Add zucchini; stir-fry 1 minute more or until crisp-tender. Add shrimp; cover and heat through. Stir in remaining lime juice and the ground red pepper. Serve in tortillas with salsa, cheese, and, if desired, greens.

Nutrition facts per serving:
267 CAL., 21 G PRO., 26 G CARBO., 9 G TOTAL FAT (3 G SAT. FAT), 124 MG CHOL., 1 G FIBER, 654 MG SODIUM.
DAILY VALUE: 26% VIT. A, 79% VIT. C, 17% CALCIUM, 22% IRON.

GARDEN VEGETABLE BURRITOS

MAKES 8 SERVINGS
TOTAL TIME: 25 MINUTES

1	cup *each:* quartered and sliced zucchini, sliced carrots, mushrooms, and red onions
1	teaspoon crushed fresh garlic
2	tablespoons Wesson® Vegetable Oil
1	14$^{1}/_{2}$-ounce can Hunt's® Choice-Cut™ Diced Tomatoes, drained
1	teaspoon dried oregano, crushed
$^{1}/_{4}$	teaspoon seasoned salt
$^{1}/_{8}$	teaspoon crushed red pepper flakes (optional)
1	16-ounce jar salsa
1	16-ounce can refried beans
8	10-inch whole wheat tortillas, warmed

In skillet sauté zucchini, carrots, mushrooms, onions, and garlic in hot Wesson Oil. Cook until vegetables are crisp-tender. Add Hunt's Choice-Cut Tomatoes, oregano, seasoned salt, red pepper, and *1 cup* salsa; simmer 3 to 5 minutes longer, then set aside.

Heat refried beans in saucepan 3 minutes. Place *$^{1}/_{4}$ cup* beans in center of each tortilla, top with *$^{1}/_{2}$ cup* vegetable-salsa mixture, and roll burrito-style. Ladle *remaining* salsa over burritos.

NUTRITION FACTS PER SERVING:
257 CAL., 8 G PRO., 40 G CARBO., 8 G TOTAL FAT (2 G SAT. FAT), 5 MG CHOL., 5 G FIBER, 995 MG SODIUM.
DAILY VALUE: 48% VIT. A, 39% VIT. C, 9% CALCIUM, 22% IRON.

JUICE BOOST

Perk up the flavor of homemade soups, chilies, and stews by adding the juice you've drained from Hunts® Choice-Cut™ Diced Tomatoes or Hunts® Whole Tomatoes. When a recipe calls for these products drained (as in the recipe above), freeze the juice in ice cube trays. Place the juice cubes in a resealable freezer bag and return the bag to the freezer. Then, as you simmer your soup or stew, just add an ice cube or two for rich tomato flavor.

PASTA & RICE

Whether you top 'em or toss 'em, pasta, rice, and grains make hearty building blocks for sensational meals. See how Hunt's® sauces lend American ease to such international favorites as pasta primavera and bulgur salad. Enjoy the full flavor Hunt's brings to pilafs, polenta, and more. So go for the grains and ladle on the Hunt's— your meals will soar to new heights of deliciousness.

Recommendation:
6 to 11 servings
from this and the bread group

Green Pea and Ham Fusilli
(see recipe, page 22)

Green Pea and Ham Fusilli

Makes 8 Servings
Total Time: 40 Minutes

2	tablespoons Wesson® Vegetable Oil
1	cup *each:* diced onion and red or orange bell peppers, cut into julienne strips
1	8-ounce package sliced fresh mushrooms
2	teaspoons crushed fresh garlic
1	14½-ounce can Hunt's® Choice-Cut™ Diced Tomatoes with Italian Style Herbs
½	pound reduced-fat, reduced-sodium ham, cut into julienne strips
1	10-ounce package frozen peas, thawed
1	6-ounce package frozen snow peas, thawed and cut in half
½	teaspoon salt
¼	teaspoon black pepper
1	tablespoon cornstarch plus 1 tablespoon water
½	pound fusilli, cooked and drained
1	cup shredded provolone cheese

In large skillet heat Wesson Oil and sauté onion, peppers, mushrooms, and garlic until crisp-tender. Add Hunt's Choice-Cut Tomatoes, ham, peas, salt, and black pepper; heat through, stirring the mixture constantly.

Move vegetables to one side of the pan, separating the broth from the vegetables; whisk broth constantly while gradually adding the cornstarch mixture. Whisk until thickened. Blend vegetables with thickened broth and cook an additional 1 minute.

Place hot cooked fusilli in a large serving bowl and top with vegetables; blend well. Serve immediately topped with provolone cheese.

Nutrition Facts per serving:
288 cal., 16 g pro., 37 g carbo., 9 g total fat (3 g sat. fat), 22 mg chol., 3 g fiber, 852 mg sodium.
Daily Value: 16% vit. A, 67% vit. C, 12% calcium, 20% iron.

Easy Pasta Primavera

MAKES 6 SERVINGS
PREPARATION TIME: 15 MINUTES • COOKING TIME: 16 MINUTES

2	tablespoons olive oil
1/4	cup *each:* chopped fresh parsley and chopped fresh basil
2	teaspoons crushed fresh garlic
1/3	cup *each:* sliced fresh mushrooms, sliced zucchini, julienne carrots, julienne yellow bell pepper, and diced onion
1	15-ounce can Hunt's® Ready Tomato Sauces Chunky Italian
1	14½-ounce can Hunt's® Choice-Cut™ Diced Tomatoes with Roasted Garlic
1	pound gemelli pasta, cooked and drained
	Grated reduced-fat Parmesan cheese for garnish
	Fresh basil sprig for garnish

In saucepan heat oil. Add parsley, basil, and garlic; sauté 2 minutes. Stir in mushrooms, zucchini, carrots, bell pepper, and onion; sauté until tender.

Add Hunt's Ready Sauce and Hunt's Choice-Cut Tomatoes; blend well. Bring sauce to boil. Reduce heat and simmer 10 minutes, uncovered. Serve over hot pasta. Garnish with grated Parmesan cheese and basil sprig.

Note: Pictured on the cover.

NUTRITION FACTS PER SERVING:
393 CAL., 12 G PRO., 68 G CARBO., 7 G TOTAL FAT (1 G SAT. FAT), 0 MG CHOL., 3 G FIBER, 649 MG SODIUM.
DAILY VALUE: 28% VIT. A, 41% VIT. C, 7% CALCIUM, 23% IRON.

LIGHTEN UP PASTA AND RICE

Make sure the pasta and rice you prepare for the recipes in this book fit a healthful diet. Omit any cooking oil, butter, margarine, or salt that's called for in the package cooking directions. The recipes are so well seasoned that you won't miss the flavor of these ingredients, and you'll cut down on calories, fat, and sodium.

Black-Eyed Pea and Pasta Salad

MAKES 4 SERVINGS
PREPARATION TIME: 30 MINUTES • CHILLING TIME: 1 HOUR

DRESSING

1/4	cup *each:* **Wesson® Vegetable or Canola Oil and red wine vinegar**
1 1/2	tablespoons country-style Dijon mustard
1	tablespoon sugar
2	teaspoons grated fresh orange peel
1	teaspoon crushed fresh garlic
3/4	teaspoon ground cumin
1/2	teaspoon salt
1/4	teaspoon cayenne pepper

SALAD

1/2	pound multi-colored wagon-wheel pasta, cooked and drained
1	15-ounce can black-eyed peas or small red beans, rinsed and drained
1	14 1/2-ounce can Hunt's® Choice-Cut™ Diced Tomatoes, undrained
2/3	cup *each:* sliced pitted black olives and chopped green or red bell pepper
1/2	cup sliced green onions
1/4	cup chopped fresh cilantro

Place Wesson Oil and *remaining* dressing ingredients in food processor or blender. Process until smooth and well blended.

In large bowl combine pasta and *remaining* ingredients. Add dressing and toss gently to mix and coat. Cover and refrigerate at least 1 hour or overnight to allow flavors to blend. Gently toss salad before serving.

Note: Give a little kick to this salad by adding red pepper flakes and hot pepper sauce. For another variation, try chopped parsley and fresh oregano instead of cilantro.

NUTRITION FACTS PER SERVING:
508 CAL., 16 G PRO., 74 G CARBO., 18 G TOTAL FAT (2 G SAT. FAT), 0 MG CHOL., 7 G FIBER, 877 MG SODIUM.
DAILY VALUE: 30% VIT. A, 91% VIT. C, 7% CALCIUM, 24% IRON.

HERBED TOMATO
PASTA PILAF

MAKES 4 SERVINGS
PREPARATION TIME: 15 MINUTES • COOKING TIME: 25 MINUTES

2   **cups sliced fresh shiitake or button mushrooms**
1   **cup thinly sliced carrots**
1   **14$\frac{1}{2}$-ounce can Hunt's® Choice-Cut™ Diced Tomatoes**
    with Italian Style Herbs, undrained
1   **8-ounce can Hunt's® Tomato Sauce**
$\frac{1}{2}$ **cup dry white wine**
1   **teaspoon sugar**
$\frac{1}{2}$ **teaspoon *each*: reduced-sodium instant beef or**
    chicken bouillon granules and fennel seed, crushed
    Dash ground red pepper
5   **cups water**
1   **cup *each*: quick-cooking barley and packaged**
    dried orzo (rosamarina)

In covered saucepan cook mushrooms and carrots in small amount of boiling water 4 minutes or until carrots are crisp-tender; drain.

Stir in Hunt's Choice-Cut Tomatoes, Hunt's Tomato Sauce, wine, sugar, bouillon granules, fennel seed, and red pepper. Bring to boil; reduce heat. Simmer, uncovered, 25 minutes or until desired consistency, stirring occasionally.

Meanwhile, in saucepan bring the 5 cups water to boil. Add barley and orzo. Cook, uncovered, 10 minutes or until tender. Drain any excess liquid. Spoon tomato mixture over barley mixture.

NUTRITION FACTS PER SERVING:
428 CAL., 14 G PRO., 86 G CARBO., 2 G TOTAL FAT (0 G SAT. FAT), 0 MG CHOL., 7 G FIBER, 964 MG SODIUM.
DAILY VALUE: 98% VIT. A, 34% VIT. C, 5% CALCIUM, 25% IRON.

Nutty Whole-Grain Bake

Makes 6 Servings
Preparation Time: 40 Minutes • Cooking Time: 40 Minutes
Standing Time: 10 Minutes

1	6$\frac{1}{2}$-ounce packet ($\frac{1}{3}$ of a 19$\frac{1}{2}$-ounce package) kashi* or 3-Grain Pilaf (see recipe below)
2	cups small broccoli flowerets
1	cup yellow summer squash, quartered lengthwise and sliced $\frac{1}{2}$ inch thick
$\frac{1}{2}$	cup chopped onion
1	cup shredded reduced-fat mozzarella cheese
$\frac{1}{2}$	cup coarsely chopped unsalted cashews or toasted almonds
$\frac{1}{4}$	cup dried currants or raisins (optional)
1	10$\frac{3}{4}$-ounce can Hunt's® Tomato Puree
$\frac{1}{3}$	cup water
$\frac{1}{2}$	teaspoon *each:* ground cumin and ground cinnamon
$\frac{1}{4}$	teaspoon *each:* ground cardamom (optional) and crushed red pepper

In saucepan prepare kashi according to package directions, *except* use 2 cups water for liquid. (Or, prepare 3-Grain Pilaf.) Meanwhile, in covered saucepan cook broccoli, squash, and onion in small amount of boiling water 2 to 3 minutes or until almost crisp-tender; drain. Stir cooked vegetables, $\frac{1}{2}$ *cup* of the cheese, the cashews, and, if desired, currants into kashi mixture.

In bowl stir together Hunt's Tomato Puree, the $\frac{1}{3}$ cup water, cumin, cinnamon, cardamom (if desired), and red pepper. Pour over kashi mixture; mix well. Transfer to 2-quart baking dish. Bake, covered, in 350° oven 35 minutes. Sprinkle with remaining cheese. Bake, uncovered, 5 minutes more. Let stand 10 minutes.

3-Grain Pilaf: In saucepan combine 1$\frac{3}{4}$ cups *water*, $\frac{1}{3}$ cup *wheat berries*, $\frac{1}{4}$ cup uncooked regular *brown rice*, and $\frac{1}{4}$ teaspoon *salt*. Bring to boil; reduce heat. Simmer, covered, 20 minutes. Stir in $\frac{1}{4}$ cup quick-cooking *barley*. Cook, covered, 10 to 15 minutes more or until rice is tender. Remove from heat. Let stand, covered, 10 minutes. Serve immediately or cover and refrigerate up to 12 hours.

*Note: Barley, sesame seeds, oats, and rice are just some of the ingredients found in kashi. Look for it in the hot cereal section of your supermarket or health food store.

Nutrition facts per serving:
270 cal., 13 g pro., 33 g carbo., 11 g total fat (3 g sat. fat), 11 mg chol., 8 g fiber, 113 mg sodium.
Daily Value: 19% vit. A, 72% vit. C, 14% calcium, 20% iron.

CHEESE POLENTA WITH TOMATO SAUCE

MAKES 4 SERVINGS
PREPARATION TIME: 25 MINUTES • CHILLING TIME: 4 HOURS
COOKING TIME: 30 MINUTES

2¼ cups water
1 cup *each:* yellow cornmeal and cold water
Dash bottled hot pepper sauce
Wesson® No-Stick Cooking Spray
1 cup shredded reduced-fat mozzarella cheese
¼ cup finely shredded Parmesan cheese
¾ cup chopped green bell pepper
1 15-ounce can Hunt's® Ready Tomato Sauces
Chunky Italian

In saucepan bring the 2¼ cups water to boil. In bowl combine cornmeal, the 1 cup cold water, and pepper sauce. Slowly add to boiling water, stirring constantly. Cook and stir until mixture returns to boil; reduce heat. Cook 10 to 15 minutes more or until very thick, stirring frequently.

Spray a 9-inch pie plate with Wesson Cooking Spray. Pour *half* of the mixture into pie plate; spread evenly. Sprinkle with mozzarella cheese and *2 tablespoons* of the Parmesan cheese. Top with green pepper. Spoon remaining cornmeal mixture over top and spread evenly. (If mixture becomes too thick, add a little water.) Sprinkle with remaining Parmesan cheese. Cover and refrigerate at least 4 hours or overnight until firm.

Bake in 400° oven 30 to 35 minutes or until golden and heated through. Meanwhile, in saucepan heat Hunt's Ready Sauce. Spoon sauce over polenta.

NUTRITION FACTS PER SERVING:
295 CAL., 15 G PRO., 35 G CARBO., 8 G TOTAL FAT (3 G SAT. FAT), 20 MG CHOL., 4 G FIBER, 821 MG SODIUM.
DAILY VALUE: 11% VIT. A, 22% VIT. C, 31% CALCIUM, 13% IRON.

POLENTA À LA SAN ANTONIO

For a change of pace, transform Italian-inspired Cheese Polenta with Tomato Sauce (see recipe above) into a sensational main dish with Tex-Mex flair. Just substitute Hunt's® Ready Tomato Sauces Chunky Chili for the Hunt's® Ready Tomato Sauces Chunky Italian.

Barley-Vegetable Medley

MAKES 6 SIDE-DISH SERVINGS
TOTAL TIME: 35 MINUTES

1	cup fresh or frozen whole kernel corn
$1/2$	cup *each:* chopped onion, chopped green bell pepper, and shredded carrot
$1/2$	cup quick-cooking barley
2	teaspoons instant reduced-sodium beef bouillon granules
$1/2$	teaspoon dried basil, crushed
$1/4$	teaspoon *each:* dried thyme and dried oregano, crushed
$1/8$	teaspoon black pepper
1	14$1/2$-ounce can Hunt's® Choice-Cut™ Diced Tomatoes, undrained

In Dutch oven bring 1$1/2$ cups *water* to boil. Stir in *first 10* ingredients, ending with black pepper. Simmer, covered, 10 minutes or until barley is tender, stirring occasionally. Drain. Stir in Hunt's Choice-Cut Tomatoes; heat through.

NUTRITION FACTS PER SERVING:
112 CAL., 4 G PRO., 24 G CARBO., 1 G TOTAL FAT (0 G SAT. FAT), 0 MG CHOL., 3 G FIBER, 463 MG SODIUM.
DAILY VALUE: 31% VIT. A, 31% VIT. C, 2% CALCIUM, 6% IRON.

Top-Notch Bulgur Salad

MAKES 4 SIDE-DISH SERVINGS
PREPARATION TIME: 25 MINUTES • CHILLING TIME: 4 HOURS

$3/4$	cup coarsely chopped, seeded cucumber
$1/2$	cup *each:* bulgur, rinsed and drained, and sliced green onion
$1/4$	cup minced fresh parsley
1	14$1/2$-ounce can Hunt's® Choice-Cut™ Diced Tomatoes
3	tablespoons fresh lemon juice
1	tablespoon olive oil
1	teaspoon dried mint, crushed
$1/8$	teaspoon garlic salt
$1/8$	teaspoon pepper

In bowl mix cucumber, bulgur, onion, and parsley. Drain Hunt's Choice-Cut Tomatoes; reserve $1/4$ cup juice. Refrigerate tomatoes. In cruet mix reserved juice, lemon juice, oil, mint, garlic salt, and pepper. Cover and shake well. Pour over bulgur mixture; toss. Cover and refrigerate 4 to 24 hours. Stir in reserved tomatoes.

NUTRITION FACTS PER SERVING:
118 CAL., 3 G PRO., 20 G CARBO., 4 G TOTAL FAT (1 G SAT. FAT), 0 MG CHOL., 5 G FIBER, 310 MG SODIUM.
DAILY VALUE: 11% VIT. A, 49% VIT. C, 3% CALCIUM, 11% IRON.

CROWD-SIZE TEX-MEX RICE

MAKES 10 SERVINGS
PREPARATION TIME: 15 MINUTES • COOKING TIME: 18 MINUTES

2¼   cups water
1   cup *each:* sliced celery and chopped onion
2   14½-ounce cans reduced-sodium, low-fat chicken broth
1   6.9-ounce package regular chicken-flavored
        rice mix with vermicelli
1   cup long grain rice
4   cups chopped cooked chicken or turkey
1   14½-ounce can Hunt's® Choice-Cut™
        Diced Tomatoes, undrained
1   4-ounce can diced green chiles, drained
2   tablespoons chopped fresh basil or 2 teaspoons
        dried basil, crushed
1   tablespoon chili powder
1   teaspoon cumin seed, crushed, or ¼ teaspoon
        ground cumin
⅛   to ¼ teaspoon black pepper
¾   cup shredded reduced-fat cheddar cheese

In Dutch oven bring *¾ cup* of the water to boil. Add celery and onion and cook, covered, 5 minutes or just until tender. *Do not drain.* Stir in chicken broth, *remaining* 1½ cups water, the rice mix and its seasoning packet, and *uncooked* long grain rice. Bring to boil; reduce heat. Simmer, covered, 15 minutes or just until rice is tender.

Gently stir in chicken, Hunt's Choice-Cut Tomatoes, chiles, basil, chili powder, cumin, and black pepper. Cook over medium-low heat until heated through, stirring occasionally. Top each serving with cheddar cheese.

NUTRITION FACTS PER SERVING:
306 CAL., 25 G PRO., 34 G CARBO., 7 G TOTAL FAT (2 G SAT. FAT), 60 MG CHOL., 1 G FIBER, 849 MG SODIUM.
DAILY VALUE: 8% VIT. A, 19% VIT. C, 9% CALCIUM, 15% IRON.

FRUITS & VEGETABLES

When counting your 3 to 5 recommended servings of fruits and vegetables, count on Hunt's®. Throughout this chapter, you'll find Hunt's makes it easy and enjoyable to "veg out." Teamed with a colorful variety of other fruits and vegetables, Hunt's tomato products make meals that brim with pleasure!

Recommendation:
2 to 4 servings of fruit
(and juice);
3 to 5 servings of vegetables

Creole Vegetable Bundles
(see recipe, page 34)

CREOLE VEGETABLE BUNDLES

MAKES 6 SIDE-DISH SERVINGS
PREPARATION TIME: 20 MINUTES • COOKING TIME: 30 MINUTES

6	large sheets of heavy aluminum foil
	Wesson® No-Stick Cooking Spray
2	cups *each:* potatoes, cut into 1-inch squares, and zucchini, cut into 1/2-inch slices
1	cup *each:* carrots, sliced 1/4 inch thick; broccoli flowerets, cut into 1-inch pieces; and sweet onion, cut into wedges
1/2	cup *each:* red bell pepper, cut into rings, and green bell pepper, cut into 1-inch pieces
1	large ear of corn, cut into 6 pieces
1	14 1/2-ounce can Hunt's® Choice-Cut™ Diced Tomatoes with Roasted Garlic, drained
3	tablespoons Wesson® Vegetable Oil
3	teaspoons Creole seasoning

Spray *each* sheet of foil with Wesson Cooking Spray. In large bowl combine *next 8* ingredients, ending with corn. Toss with Hunt's Choice-Cut Tomatoes and Wesson Oil.

Evenly divide vegetable mixture among prepared foil sheets. Sprinkle *1/2 teaspoon* Creole seasoning on *each* vegetable packet. Bring sides of foil to center and fold over to seal. Fold ends to center, creating a tight bundle. Repeat with *remaining* packets.

Place bundles on cookie sheets and bake at 425° for 30 minutes. Careful now! Put on those oven mitts to avoid that escaping steam.

NUTRITION FACTS PER SERVING:
173 CAL., 4 G PRO., 26 G CARBO., 8 G TOTAL FAT (1 G SAT. FAT), 0 MG CHOL., 4 G FIBER, 406 MG SODIUM.
DAILY VALUE: 67% VIT. A, 77% VIT. C, 4% CALCIUM, 11% IRON.

VERSATILE VEGGIES

You can turn Creole Vegetable Bundles (see recipe above) into a whole new side dish simply by changing the vegetables and the type of Hunt's® Choice-Cut™ Diced Tomatoes you use. Next time, include yellow summer squash in place of the zucchini, orange and yellow bell peppers instead of red and green, and cauliflower flowerets rather than broccoli. Then, substitute Hunt's® Choice-Cut™ Diced Tomatoes with Italian Style Herbs for the Hunt's® Choice-Cut™ Diced Tomatoes with Roasted Garlic. You'll be delighted with the colorful and delicious results.

SCALLOPED TOMATOES

MAKES 4 SIDE-DISH SERVINGS
PREPARATION TIME: 30 MINUTES • COOKING TIME: 20 MINUTES

3	slices bread, toasted
2	tablespoons margarine or butter
1/2	cup *each:* chopped celery and chopped onion
1	14 1/2-ounce can Hunt's® Choice-Cut™ Diced Tomatoes, undrained
2	tablespoons water
1	tablespoon all-purpose flour
1 1/2	teaspoons chopped fresh marjoram or basil; or 1/2 teaspoon dried marjoram or basil, crushed
1	teaspoon sugar
1/4	teaspoon salt
1/8	teaspoon pepper
	Grated reduced-fat Parmesan cheese (optional)

Spread toast with *1 tablespoon* of the margarine. Cut toast into cubes; set aside.

In large skillet cook celery and onion in remaining margarine until crisp-tender. Stir in Hunt's Choice-Cut Tomatoes. Bring to boil; reduce heat. Simmer, covered, 8 minutes.

In small bowl stir together water, flour, marjoram, sugar, salt, and pepper; add to tomato mixture. Cook and stir until thick and bubbly. Stir *two-thirds* of the toast cubes into tomato mixture. Pour into 1-quart casserole.

Top with remaining toast cubes. If desired, sprinkle with cheese. Bake in 350° oven 20 minutes or until bubbly.

NUTRITION FACTS PER SERVING:
142 CAL., 3 G PRO., 18 G CARBO., 7 G TOTAL FAT (1 G SAT. FAT), 0 MG CHOL., 2 G FIBER, 952 MG SODIUM.
DAILY VALUE: 13% VIT. A, 28% VIT. C, 5% CALCIUM, 9% IRON.

SOUTHWESTERN STUFFED SQUASH

MAKES 4 TO 8 SERVINGS
TOTAL TIME: 30 MINUTES

8	small crookneck squash, small zucchini, and/or medium pattypan squash
1	tablespoon Wesson® Vegetable Oil
1/3	cup *each:* chopped fresh cilantro, red onion, and shredded carrots
1/2	teaspoon *each:* crushed fresh garlic and ground cumin
1	16-ounce can low-fat refried beans with green chile and lime*
1	14½-ounce can Hunt's® Choice-Cut™ Diced Tomatoes with Crushed Red Pepper and Basil, drained
3/4	cup shredded reduced-fat pepper-jack cheese
1	2½-ounce can sliced pitted black olives, drained and cut in half

Halve crookneck squash and zucchini; remove tops from pattypan squash. Scoop out pulp and discard, leaving 1/4 inch around shell. In pot of boiling water blanch squash 3 to 5 minutes or until tender.

Remove and place in bowl of cold water to stop cooking process. In same pan heat Wesson Oil. Add cilantro, onion, carrots, garlic, and cumin; sauté until carrots are tender. Stir in beans, Hunt's Choice-Cut Tomatoes, 1/3 *cup* cheese, and olives; heat through.

Place squash on cookie sheet; stuff with bean mixture. Sprinkle *remaining* cheese over squash; broil until cheese is melted. Garnish with additional cilantro.

Note: If you can't find low-fat refried beans with green chile and lime, substitute fat-free or regular refried beans.

NUTRITION FACTS PER SERVING:
293 CAL., 15 G PRO., 33 G CARBO., 12 G TOTAL FAT (3 G SAT. FAT), 18 MG CHOL., 4 G FIBER, 769 MG SODIUM.
DAILY VALUE: 44% VIT. A, 43% VIT. C, 25% CALCIUM, 18% IRON.

Easy-on-the-Waistline Eggplant Bake

MAKES 8 SIDE-DISH SERVINGS
PREPARATION TIME: 15 MINUTES • COOKING TIME: 30 MINUTES

	Wesson® No-Stick Cooking Spray
3	tablespoons Wesson® Canola Oil
4	cups peeled and cubed eggplant, cut into 1½-inch pieces
½	cup diced onion
1	14½-ounce can Hunt's® Choice-Cut™ Diced Tomatoes with Italian Style Herbs, undrained
2	tablespoons finely chopped fresh parsley
¾	teaspoon *each:* sugar and salt
⅛	teaspoon pepper
1	cup fat-free, seasoned large croutons, slightly crushed
½	cup *each:* shredded provolone and reduced-fat cheddar cheese, combined

Spray 11x7x2-inch baking dish with Wesson Cooking Spray. Preheat oven to 350°.

In large skillet heat *2 tablespoons* Wesson Oil until hot. Sauté eggplant 5 to 7 minutes or until tender; spoon into dish.

In same skillet heat *remaining* oil and sauté onion. Stir in Hunt's Choice-Cut Tomatoes, parsley, sugar, salt, and pepper; bring to boil. Evenly pour tomato mixture over eggplant. Top with croutons and cheeses. Bake, uncovered, 30 minutes or until cheeses are brown and juices are bubbly.

NUTRITION FACTS PER SERVING:
180 CAL., 7 G PRO., 13 G CARBO., 11 G TOTAL FAT (3 G SAT. FAT), 13 MG CHOL., 3 G FIBER, 821 MG SODIUM.
DAILY VALUE: 9% VIT. A, 21% VIT. C, 14% CALCIUM, 4% IRON.

SPICY TOMATO PESTO

$1^{1}/_{2}$ cups *each:* firmly packed fresh basil leaves and torn
fresh spinach leaves, washed
1 $14^{1}/_{2}$-ounce can Hunt's® Choice-Cut™ Diced Tomatoes
with Crushed Red Pepper and Basil, drained and
liquid reserved
$^{2}/_{3}$ cup grated reduced-fat Parmesan cheese
$^{1}/_{3}$ cup toasted pine nuts
1 tablespoon crushed fresh garlic
$^{1}/_{4}$ teaspoon salt
$^{1}/_{4}$ teaspoon crushed red pepper flakes
1 tablespoon fresh lemon juice
$^{1}/_{2}$ pound angel hair pasta, cooked and drained

In blender or food processor combine basil, spinach, $^{1}/_{3}$ can Hunt's Choice-Cut Tomatoes, $^{1}/_{3}$ cup reserved tomato liquid, cheese, $^{1}/_{4}$ cup pine nuts, garlic, salt, pepper flakes, and lemon juice. On high speed, puree ingredients 10 seconds. Stop machine and scrape sides down; cover. Press pulse switch on and off to process to a fine diced consistency. *Do not puree.* Spoon pesto into small bowl; fold in *remaining* tomatoes.

Spoon *half* of the pesto over hot pasta; toss until well coated. Refrigerate or freeze *remaining* pesto for another use (see tip below). Garnish with *remaining* pine nuts and additional Parmesan cheese.

NUTRITION FACTS PER SERVING:
205 CAL., 7 G PRO., 37 G CARBO., 3 G TOTAL FAT (0 G SAT. FAT), 0 MG CHOL., 1 G FIBER, 322 MG SODIUM.
DAILY VALUE: 7% VIT. A, 13% VIT. C, 3% CALCIUM, 14% IRON.

PESTO ON CALL

Spicy Tomato Pesto (see recipe above) is perfect on pasta, but don't stop there. Put the remaining pesto to good use by adding it to soups or stews, using it as a stuffing for fish, tucking it into chicken rolls, or dolloping it on pizza. Store the pesto in a covered container in the refrigerator for up to 3 days. Or, spoon it into 1-tablespoon portions on a baking sheet (or into ice cube trays). Freeze the portions until firm and place them in a resealable freezer bag. Store the portions in the freezer for up to 1 month. Then use the pesto a few portions at a time.

CHUNKY MUSHROOM TOMATO SAUCE

MAKES 8 SIDE-DISH SERVINGS
PREPARATION TIME: 20 MINUTES • COOKING TIME: 30 MINUTES

$^1/_4$	cup Wesson® Best Blend Oil
$^1/_2$	pound sliced fresh mushrooms
1	cup chopped onions
$^1/_4$	cup *each:* chopped fresh parsley and fresh basil, lightly packed
1	tablespoon crushed fresh garlic
3	14$^1/_2$-ounce cans Hunt's® Whole Tomatoes, undrained and crushed
1	8-ounce can Hunt's® Tomato Sauce
1	6-ounce can Hunt's® Tomato Paste
$^1/_8$	teaspoon pepper
2	2$^1/_2$-pound spaghetti squash, cooked according to directions*
	Shaved Parmesan cheese for garnish

In Dutch oven in hot Wesson Oil, sauté mushrooms, onions, parsley, basil, and garlic until onions are tender. Stir in *next 4* ingredients, ending with pepper. Simmer, covered, 30 minutes or until slightly thickened. Stir often. Serve over hot cooked spaghetti squash. Garnish with shaved Parmesan cheese.

To cook squash: Halve squash lengthwise; remove seeds. Place, cut sides down, in 2 baking dishes with $^1/_4$ cup *water* in each dish. Microwave, covered, on 100% power (high) 15 to 20 minutes or until tender, rearranging once. Remove pulp from shells.

Note: If desired, make this sauce days or weeks before serving. Cool and place in an airtight container and refrigerate no more than 5 days or freeze up to 3 months.

NUTRITION FACTS PER SERVING:
165 CAL., 4 G PRO., 22 G CARBO., 8 G TOTAL FAT (1 G SAT. FAT), 0 MG CHOL., 5 G FIBER, 496 MG SODIUM.
DAILY VALUE: 20% VIT. A, 76% VIT. C, 6% CALCIUM, 19% IRON.

MIKE'S SENSATIONAL SALSA

MAKES 12 APPETIZER SERVINGS
PREPARATION TIME: 15 MINUTES • CHILLING TIME: 2 HOURS
STANDING TIME: 30 MINUTES

2	14½-ounce cans Hunt's® Choice-Cut™ Diced Tomatoes, *1* can drained
¼	cup sliced green onion (white and green portions)
3	tablespoons chopped onion
2	tablespoons chopped fresh cilantro (optional)
1	tablespoon diced green chiles
2	teaspoons diced canned or fresh jalapeño peppers, seeds included (see tip below)
1½	teaspoons sugar
1	teaspoon crushed fresh garlic
¼	teaspoon *each:* salt, ground cumin, and hot pepper sauce
	Baked tortilla chips or cut fresh vegetables

In medium bowl combine Hunt's Choice-Cut Tomatoes and *next 10* ingredients, ending with hot pepper sauce. Cover and refrigerate *at least* 2 hours or overnight. Remove a half hour before serving. Stir once before serving and serve with chips or vegetables.

NUTRITION FACTS PER ¼ CUP:
18 CAL., 1 G PRO., 4 G CARBO., 0 G TOTAL FAT (0 G SAT. FAT), 0 MG CHOL., 1 G FIBER, 209 MG SODIUM.
DAILY VALUE: 4% VIT. A, 21% VIT. C, 1% CALCIUM, 3% IRON.

CHILE POINTER

Working with hot chile peppers such as jalapeños and serranos requires a little extra care. The oils from the peppers can burn your skin and eyes. When seeding or chopping hot peppers, be sure to wear rubber gloves (or slip a plastic bag over each hand). Don't touch or rub your eyes while you're working. After you've finished, wash your hands and nails thoroughly with soap and water to remove any oils that may remain on your hands.

Hunt's Famous French Salad Dressing

MAKES 2 CUPS DRESSING
PREPARATION TIME: 10 MINUTES • CHILLING TIME: 30 MINUTES

1	8-ounce can Hunt's® Tomato Sauce
1/4	cup Wesson® Vegetable Oil
1/3	cup rice vinegar
1	tablespoon light brown sugar
1/2	teaspoon salt
1/4	teaspoon dry mustard
1/8	teaspoon garlic powder
	Garden salad or cut fresh vegetables

Combine *first 7* ingredients in cruet or jar, ending with garlic powder. Cover and shake well; refrigerate at least 30 minutes. Shake well before serving. Serve on a garden salad or with fresh vegetables.

NUTRITION FACTS PER TABLESPOON:
18 CAL., 0 G PRO., 1 G CARBO., 2 G TOTAL FAT (0 G SAT. FAT), 0 MG CHOL., 0 G FIBER, 78 MG SODIUM.
DAILY VALUE: 0% VIT. A, 1% VIT. C, 0% CALCIUM, 0% IRON.

Creamy Tomato and Herb Salad Dressing

MAKES 3 CUPS DRESSING
PREPARATION TIME: 15 MINUTES • CHILLING TIME: 1 HOUR

1	14½-ounce can Hunt's® Choice-Cut™ Diced Tomatoes with Roasted Garlic, undrained
1/4	cup *each:* cider vinegar and light mayonnaise dressing
1/4	cup chopped fresh parsley
2	tablespoons *each:* chopped fresh basil and spicy brown mustard
1	teaspoon *each:* sugar and crushed fresh garlic
1/4	cup Wesson® Vegetable Oil
	Garden salad or cut fresh vegetables

Puree *first 8* ingredients in food processor 20 seconds. Pulse food processor on and off (about 10 seconds) while gradually adding Wesson® Oil. Salt and pepper to taste. Cover and refrigerate 1 hour. May be prepared the day before. Shake well before serving. Serve on a garden salad or try as a dip with fresh vegetables.

NUTRITION FACTS PER TABLESPOON:
17 CAL., 0 G PRO., 1 G CARBO., 2 G TOTAL FAT (0 G SAT. FAT), 0 MG CHOL., 0 G FIBER, 56 MG SODIUM.
DAILY VALUE: 0% VIT. A, 2% VIT. C, 0% CALCIUM, 0% IRON.

Italian Vegetable Soup Made Easy

Makes 10 Side-Dish Servings
Preparation Time: 15 Minutes • Cooking Time: 15 Minutes

1	cup diced onion
3/4	cup sliced celery
2	tablespoons Wesson® Vegetable Oil
4	14½-ounce cans reduced-sodium, low-fat chicken broth
2	14½-ounce cans Hunt's® Stewed Tomatoes, undrained
1/2	teaspoon *each:* garlic powder, salt, and fines herbes seasoning
1/8	teaspoon pepper
1	16-ounce bag frozen mixed Italian vegetables
1	15½-ounce can red kidney beans, drained
1/3	cup long grain rice, uncooked
	Fresh marjoram sprigs for garnish

In large Dutch oven sauté onion and celery in hot Wesson Oil until crisp-tender. Stir in *next 6* ingredients, ending with pepper; bring to a boil. Add vegetables, beans, and rice. Reduce heat, cover, and simmer 15 to 20 minutes or until rice is cooked and vegetables are tender. Garnish with marjoram sprigs.

Nutrition facts per serving:
141 cal., 6 g pro., 25 g carbo., 3 g total fat (0 g sat. fat), 0 mg chol., 4 g fiber, 497 mg sodium.
Daily Value: 27% vit. A, 34% vit. C, 5% calcium, 11% iron.

Keeping Salt in Check

Trying to cook with less salt? If so, Hunt's® No Salt Added products are just what you need. You can make mouthwatering lower-sodium meals with the no-salt-added versions of stewed tomatoes, whole tomatoes, tomato sauce, and tomato paste. Just substitute them for the regular products listed in your recipes. Then, if you like, boost the flavor a bit by increasing the other seasonings slightly.

DAIRY PRODUCTS

Say cheese! And include cheese and other dairy foods in your meals every day. The trick to healthful dairy-based recipes lies in selecting low-fat or nonfat milk, cheese, sour cream, and yogurt. And the secret to keeping slimmed-down recipes full of rich taste lies in choosing Hunt's® tomato products. With Hunt's, you can skim the milk and milk products without skimping on flavor!

Recommendation:
2 to 3 servings a day

Summer Vegetable Lasagna
(see recipe, page 48)

SUMMER VEGETABLE LASAGNA

MAKES 10 SERVINGS
PREPARATION TIME: 1 HOUR • COOKING TIME: 1 HOUR
STANDING TIME: 10 MINUTES

SAUCE AND VEGETABLES

2 **15-ounce cans Hunt's® Ready Tomato Sauces Original Italian**
1 **teaspoon** *each:* **dried basil, crushed, and Italian seasoning**
1 **tablespoon crushed fresh garlic**
6 **large fresh basil leaves, minced**
2 **tablespoons Wesson® Vegetable Oil Wesson® No-Stick Cooking Spray**
1 **medium eggplant, peeled and cut into ¼-inch slices**
2 **medium zucchini, cut lengthwise into ¼-inch slices**
2 **medium onions, cut into ¼-inch slices**
2 **medium red or yellow bell peppers, cored and cut in half lengthwise**
⅛ **teaspoon dried minced onion Dash garlic powder**

LASAGNA

1 **15-ounce carton low-fat ricotta cheese**
½ **cup grated reduced-fat Parmesan cheese**
2 **eggs**
9 **lasagna noodles, cooked, rinsed, and drained**
2 **cups shredded reduced-fat mozzarella cheese**

Sauce and Vegetables: Combine Hunt's Ready Sauce, dried basil, and seasoning. Simmer 30 minutes, stirring occasionally. In small bowl combine garlic, fresh basil, and Wesson Oil; set aside.

Spray 3 baking sheets with Wesson Cooking Spray. Arrange eggplant on *1* baking sheet; brush with garlic mixture. Arrange *remaining* vegetables on *remaining* sheets; sprinkle with dried onion and garlic powder. Broil *all* vegetables until skins of peppers are charred and other vegetables are roasted, turning as needed. Remove skins from peppers.

Lasagna: In bowl mix ricotta, Parmesan cheese, and eggs. Spray 13x9x2-inch baking dish with Wesson Cooking Spray; spread *1 cup* sauce on bottom. Layer *3* noodles, *⅔* cup sauce, *½* ricotta mixture, and *all* eggplant. Top with *⅔ cup* sauce, *1 cup* mozzarella, *all* onion, another *⅔ cup* sauce, and *remaining* ricotta mixture. Layer *3* more noodles, *⅔ cup* sauce, *all* zucchini, and *all* roasted peppers; top with *remaining 3* noodles and sauce.

Bake, covered, at 350° 50 minutes. Uncover and top with *remaining* mozzarella cheese. Bake an additional 10 minutes until bubbly. Let stand 10 minutes.

NUTRITION FACTS PER SERVING:
287 CAL., 17 G PRO., 32 G CARBO., 10 G TOTAL FAT (3 G SAT. FAT), 62 MG CHOL., 3 G FIBER, 635 MG SODIUM.
DAILY VALUE: 28% VIT. A, 57% VIT. C, 22% CALCIUM, 13% IRON.

SOUTH-OF-THE-BORDER LASAGNA

MAKES 8 SERVINGS
PREPARATION TIME: 30 MINUTES • COOKING TIME: 40 MINUTES
STANDING TIME: 10 MINUTES

	Wesson® No-Stick Cooking Spray
¹/₂	cup *each*: chopped onion and chopped green bell pepper
1	teaspoon crushed fresh garlic
2	15-ounce cans black beans, rinsed and drained
2	15-ounce cans Hunt's® Tomato Sauce
¹/₄	cup chopped fresh cilantro
1	12-ounce carton low-fat cottage cheese
1	8-ounce package reduced-fat cream cheese (Neufchâtel), softened
¹/₄	cup light dairy sour cream
9	packaged dried lasagna noodles, cooked and drained

For sauce, spray unheated no stick skillet with Wesson Cooking Spray. Add onion, bell pepper, and garlic and cook until tender.

Mash *1 can* of the beans. Stir the mashed beans, the remaining can of *unmashed* beans, the Hunt's Tomato Sauce, and cilantro into vegetables; heat through.

Combine cottage cheese, cream cheese, and sour cream. Rinse cooked noodles with cold water; drain again.

Spray 13x9x2-inch baking dish with cooking spray. Arrange *3* noodles in dish. Top with *one-third* of the sauce and *one-third* of the cheese mixture. Repeat layers twice, *except* reserve remaining cheese mixture.

Bake, covered, in 350° oven 40 to 45 minutes or until heated through. Top with reserved cheese mixture. Let stand 10 minutes.

NUTRITION FACTS PER SERVING:
300 CAL., 19 G PRO., 41 G CARBO., 8 G TOTAL FAT (5 G SAT. FAT), 25 MG CHOL., 7 G FIBER, 1,222 MG SODIUM.
DAILY VALUE: 22% VIT. A, 35% VIT. C, 9% CALCIUM, 21% IRON.

GOOD LOOKIN' LASAGNA

For picture-perfect lasagna, it's important to keep the lasagna noodles from either sticking together or tearing as you pull them apart. To avoid sticking, drain the noodles in a colander and rinse with cold water. Then, arrange them in a single layer on foil until you're ready to start layering. Fit noodles into the dish by trimming them with kitchen scissors or a knife and overlapping them slightly.

Mushroom-Artichoke Strata

MAKES 6 SERVINGS
PREPARATION TIME: 20 MINUTES • CHILLING TIME: 8 HOURS
COOKING TIME: 50 MINUTES • STANDING TIME: 10 MINUTES

1/4	cup reduced-sodium, low-fat chicken broth
2	cups sliced fresh mushrooms
1	9-ounce package frozen artichoke hearts, thawed and chopped
1/2	of a 10-ounce package frozen chopped spinach, thawed and well drained
1	15-ounce carton fat-free ricotta cheese
1/4	cup grated reduced-fat Parmesan cheese
1 1/2	teaspoons chopped fresh basil or 1/2 teaspoon dried basil, crushed
1 1/2	teaspoons chopped fresh thyme or 1/2 teaspoon dried thyme, crushed
1 1/2	cups skim milk
2	eggs
2	egg whites
1/4	teaspoon *each:* ground nutmeg and pepper
	Wesson® No-Stick Cooking Spray
8	thin slices whole wheat or sourdough bread, halved
1	15-ounce can Hunt's® Ready Tomato Sauces Chunky Italian

In saucepan bring chicken broth to boil. Add mushrooms and simmer, uncovered, 3 minutes; drain. In bowl toss together cooked mushrooms, artichoke hearts, and spinach. In second bowl combine ricotta and Parmesan cheeses, basil, and thyme. In third bowl whisk together milk, eggs, egg whites, nutmeg, and pepper.

Spray 11x7x2-inch baking dish with Wesson Cooking Spray. Arrange *8 halved* bread slices in dish. Top with spinach mixture, then ricotta mixture. Arrange *remaining* 8 halved bread slices on top. Pour egg mixture slowly over bread, using spatula to press down on bread until egg mixture is absorbed. Cover and refrigerate 8 to 24 hours.

Bake in 350° oven 50 to 60 minutes or until set and golden brown. Let stand 10 minutes. Meanwhile, in saucepan heat Hunt's Ready Sauce. Serve with strata.

NUTRITION FACTS PER SERVING:
275 CAL., 22 G PRO., 38 G CARBO., 5 G TOTAL FAT (1 G SAT. FAT), 80 MG CHOL., 4 G FIBER, 795 MG SODIUM.
DAILY VALUE: 39% VIT. A, 12% VIT. C, 29% CALCIUM, 20% IRON.

GREEK PASTA CASSEROLE

MAKES 6 SERVINGS
PREPARATION TIME: 25 MINUTES • COOKING TIME: 45 MINUTES
STANDING TIME: 5 MINUTES

	Wesson® No-Stick Cooking Spray
3/4	pound extra lean ground beef
1	teaspoon crushed fresh garlic
1	15-ounce can Hunt's® Ready Tomato Sauces Original Italian
1/3	cup fresh basil leaves, cut into strips
1/2	teaspoon salt
2	cups radiatore pasta, cooked and drained
1	2½-ounce can sliced pitted black olives, drained
1	4-ounce package crumbled feta cheese with crushed peppercorns
1½	cups skim milk
4	eggs

Spray 8x8x2-inch baking dish with Wesson Cooking Spray; set aside. Preheat oven to 350°. In 10-inch skillet cook ground beef and garlic until browned; drain. Stir in Hunt's Ready Sauce, *1/4 cup* of the basil, and salt; blend well. Fold in cooked pasta and olives.

Spread mixture into baking dish; sprinkle evenly with cheese. In small bowl beat together milk and eggs; pour over casserole. Bake, uncovered, 45 to 55 minutes or until knife inserted in center comes out clean. Let stand 5 minutes. Garnish with *remaining* basil.

NUTRITION FACTS PER SERVING:
356 CAL., 24 G PRO., 29 G CARBO., 17 G TOTAL FAT (6 G SAT. FAT), 196 MG CHOL., 2 G FIBER, 848 MG SODIUM.
DAILY VALUE: 22% VIT. A, 10% VIT. C, 17% CALCIUM, 22% IRON.

MIX-AND-MATCH PASTA

Although deeply-ridged radiatore pasta gives a company-special look to Greek Pasta Casserole (see recipe above), you can make this hearty dish with several other pasta shapes. Elbow macaroni, wagon wheels, medium shells, or corkscrew macaroni are all good choices.

CHILE RELLENOS CASSEROLE

MAKES 6 SERVINGS
PREPARATION TIME: 20 MINUTES • COOKING TIME: 30 MINUTES
STANDING TIME: 5 MINUTES

1	cup evaporated skim milk
3/4	cup refrigerated or frozen egg product, thawed, or 3 eggs
1/3	cup all-purpose flour
1 1/2	cups shredded reduced-fat cheddar cheese
1/2	cup shredded reduced-fat Monterey Jack cheese Wesson® No-Stick Cooking Spray
3	4 1/2-ounce cans whole green chiles
1	8-ounce can Hunt's® Tomato Sauce

In bowl beat milk, egg product, and flour until smooth. Mix cheeses, reserving 1/2 cup. Spray 11x7x2-inch baking dish with Wesson Cooking Spray. Rinse, drain, and seed chiles; arrange *half* of the chiles in dish. Sprinkle with *half* of the remaining cheese; add *half* of the milk mixture. Repeat layers. Pour Hunt's Tomato Sauce over top. Bake in 350° oven 30 to 35 minutes or just until set. Sprinkle with reserved 1/2 cup cheese. Let stand 5 minutes.

NUTRITION FACTS PER SERVING:
222 CAL., 20 G PRO., 15 G CARBO., 9 G TOTAL FAT (4 G SAT. FAT), 28 MG CHOL., 1 G FIBER, 758 MG SODIUM.
DAILY VALUE: 21% VIT. A, 40% VIT. C, 40% CALCIUM, 11% IRON.

CHEESY CHILI DIP

MAKES 12 APPETIZER SERVINGS
TOTAL TIME: 20 MINUTES

1	16-ounce can low-fat refried black beans
1	15-ounce can Hunt's® Ready Tomato Sauces Chunky Chili
1	cup *each:* shredded reduced-fat Cheddar cheese and shredded reduced-fat pepper-jack cheese
1	4-ounce can diced green chiles
1	tablespoon chopped fresh cilantro
1/2	teaspoon ground cumin Baked tortilla chips or cut fresh vegetables

In large saucepan combine *all* ingredients *except* chips or vegetables; mix well. On medium-low heat cook until heated through or until cheese has melted. Serve with tortilla chips or vegetables.

NUTRITION FACTS PER SERVING:
109 CAL., 8 G PRO., 10 G CARBO., 4 G TOTAL FAT (2 G SAT. FAT), 16 MG CHOL., 2 G FIBER, 497 MG SODIUM.
DAILY VALUE: 3% VIT. A, 23% VIT. C, 13% CALCIUM, 7% IRON.

CLASSIC SOUTHWEST CASSEROLE

MAKES 6 TO 8 SERVINGS
PREPARATION TIME: 35 MINUTES • COOKING TIME: 30 MINUTES
STANDING TIME: 10 MINUTES

1	14½-ounce can Hunt's® Choice-Cut™ Diced Tomatoes
2	cups chopped onion
1	15-ounce can Hunt's® Ready Tomato Sauces Chunky Chili
1	14½-ounce can Hunt's® Choice-Cut™ Diced Tomatoes with Crushed Red Pepper and Basil, undrained
1½	cups chopped green bell pepper
1	4-ounce can diced green chiles
1	teaspoon *each:* ground cumin and crushed fresh garlic (optional)
2	15-ounce cans black beans or red kidney beans, rinsed and drained
1	cup frozen whole kernel corn
½	cup chopped fresh cilantro
12	6-inch corn tortillas
1½	cups shredded reduced-fat Monterey Jack cheese
½	cup light dairy sour cream or plain low-fat yogurt (optional)

Drain Hunt's Choice-Cut Tomatoes, reserving juice. Set tomatoes aside. In skillet combine reserved juice, onion, and *next 6* ingredients, ending with garlic. Bring to boil; reduce heat. Simmer, uncovered, 15 minutes. Transfer to very large bowl. Stir in beans, corn, and ¼ *cup* of the cilantro.

Spread *one-third* of the bean mixture over bottom of a 13x9x2-inch baking dish. Top with 6 tortillas, overlapping as necessary, and ¾ *cup* cheese. Add another *one-third* of the bean mixture; top with *remaining* tortillas and *remaining* bean mixture.

Bake, covered, in 350° oven 30 to 35 minutes or until heated through. Sprinkle with *remaining* cheese. Let stand 10 minutes. Top with reserved tomatoes and *remaining* cilantro. If desired, serve with sour cream.

NUTRITION FACTS PER SERVING:
387 CAL., 24 G PRO., 66 G CARBO., 8 G TOTAL FAT (3 G SAT. FAT), 20 MG CHOL., 9 G FIBER, 1,532 MG SODIUM.
DAILY VALUE: 16% VIT. A, 109% VIT. C, 34% CALCIUM, 25% IRON.

DAIRY PRODUCTS

MEAT

With the Hunt's® tomato products in this tempting array of roasts, stews, steaks, and more, a little meat goes a long way. That's because Hunt's brings out the rich, full flavors in all you cook, making flavor—not fat—the main event of the meal. Whether stewed, simmered, roasted, or grilled, these recipes make meats cook up tasty and tender in no time—thanks to Hunt's.

Recommendation:
2 to 3 servings a day from this and the other protein group

Hawaiian-Style Pot Roast
(see recipe, page 58)

Hawaiian-Style Pot Roast

MAKES 10 SERVINGS
PREPARATION TIME: 20 MINUTES • COOKING TIME: 2 HOURS

1	tablespoon Wesson® Vegetable Oil
1	3- to 4-pound boneless beef roast, trimmed
4	large potatoes, washed and cut into 1½-inch cubes
2	cups *each:* onion, sliced into wedges; cubed red or green bell pepper; and sliced celery
1	teaspoon crushed fresh garlic
1	15-ounce can Hunt's® Ready Tomato Sauces Chunky Special
1	8¼-ounce can pineapple chunks in heavy syrup, liquid reserved
¼	cup packed brown sugar
3	tablespoons Worcestershire sauce
2	tablespoons apple cider vinegar
1	tablespoon cornstarch

Preheat oven to 375°. In large skillet heat Wesson Oil; brown roast on all sides. Place roast in large roasting pan along with potatoes; set aside.

In same skillet with drippings, sauté *all vegetables* and garlic until crisp-tender. Stir in Hunt's Ready Sauce, pineapple chunks, brown sugar, Worcestershire sauce, and vinegar; heat through.

Pour mixture over roast and potatoes. Cover and bake 2 hours or until desired doneness. Transfer meat and vegetables to serving platter.

In small bowl combine reserved pineapple syrup and cornstarch; mix until cornstarch is dissolved. Slowly whisk mixture into juices; cook and stir until thickened and bubbly. Cook and stir 2 minutes more. Serve with meat and vegetables.

NUTRITION FACTS PER SERVING:
447 CAL., 33 G PRO., 41 G CARBO., 17 G TOTAL FAT (6 G SAT. FAT), 101 MG CHOL., 3 G FIBER, 331 MG SODIUM.
DAILY VALUE: 9% VIT. A, 78% VIT. C, 5% CALCIUM, 35% IRON.

SASSY SKILLET SUPPER

This four-ingredient recipe makes a mouthwatering main dish in next to no time. In a large skillet brown 1 pound of lean *ground beef* or *pork*; drain. Stir in one 14½-ounce can *Hunts® Stewed Tomatoes,* undrained; one 8-ounce can *whole kernel corn,* undrained; and a 3-ounce package of *Oriental noodles with pork flavor.* (Break up the noodles, if you like.) Simmer, covered, 10 minutes or until noodles are tender and liquid is absorbed. Makes 4 servings.

FIRE CHIEF'S MARINATED FLANK STEAK

MAKES 8 SERVINGS
PREPARATION TIME: 15 MINUTES • MARINATING TIME: 2 HOURS
COOKING TIME: 12 MINUTES

6	dried pasilla or ancho chile peppers, seeds removed and cut into strips (optional)
1	cup coarsely chopped onion
1	tablespoon crushed fresh garlic
2	tablespoons Wesson® Best Blend or Vegetable Oil
1	8-ounce can Hunt's® Tomato Sauce
1/4	cup water
2	tablespoons fresh lime juice
2 1/2	teaspoons cumin seed
1	teaspoon brown sugar
3/4	teaspoon salt
1/4	teaspoon reduced-sodium instant beef bouillon granules
2	1- to 1 1/2-pound beef flank steaks, trimmed and tenderized
2	fresh limes

In medium skillet over medium-low heat, sauté chiles, onion, and garlic in Wesson Oil until onion is tender. Do not drain. Pour sautéed mixture into blender. Add Hunt's Tomato Sauce and *remaining* ingredients *except* steaks and fresh limes; blend to a smooth, thick sauce.

Marinate steaks in refrigerator 2 hours in *half* the marinade. Reserve remaining marinade; set aside.

Over hot coals grill steaks while continuously basting with *one-third* of the reserved marinade. Grill to desired doneness. Before serving, generously squeeze with fresh lime juice and brush steaks with *remaining* marinade.

Note: Makes a great steak sandwich or fajitas. For fajitas, after grilling, cut steaks into thin strips and serve with warm tortillas, reduced-fat cheese, guacamole, and light sour cream.

NUTRITION FACTS PER SERVING:
250 CAL., 24 G PRO., 9 G CARBO., 14 G TOTAL FAT (4 G SAT. FAT), 53 MG CHOL., 1 G FIBER, 477 MG SODIUM.
DAILY VALUE: 4% VIT. A, 12% VIT. C, 8% CALCIUM, 55% IRON.

Fiesta Meatloaf

MAKES 10 SERVINGS
PREPARATION TIME: 15 MINUTES • COOKING TIME: 1 HOUR 10 MINUTES
STANDING TIME: 10 MINUTES

1½	pounds lean ground beef
1	15-ounce can Hunt's® Ready Tomato Sauces Original Meatloaf Fixin's
2	teaspoons chili powder
½	teaspoon *each:* ground cumin and garlic powder
1¼	cups crushed corn chips or baked tortilla chips
½	cup *each:* chopped onion and green olives stuffed with pimientos, chopped
⅓	cup frozen Mexican-style corn, thawed
1	4-ounce can diced green chiles
2	eggs, lightly beaten

Preheat oven to 375°. In large bowl combine meat, *1 cup* Hunt's Ready Sauce, *1 teaspoon* chili powder, *¼ teaspoon* cumin, *¼ teaspoon* garlic powder, and *remaining* ingredients. Blend well, avoiding overmixing.

Firmly pack meat mixture into 9x5x3-inch loaf pan; shape into loaf. Bake, uncovered, 1 hour; drain.

Meanwhile, combine *remaining* ready sauce, chili powder, cumin, and garlic powder; blend well. Generously spread sauce mixture over meatloaf; bake an additional 10 minutes. Let stand 10 minutes before serving. Garnish with additional corn and quartered olives.

NUTRITION FACTS PER SERVING:
218 CAL., 16 G PRO., 10 G CARBO., 13 G TOTAL FAT (4 G SAT. FAT), 85 MG CHOL., 1 G FIBER, 622 MG SODIUM.
DAILY VALUE: 7% VIT. A, 11% VIT. C, 3% CALCIUM, 13% IRON.

Midwest Swiss Steak

Makes 6 Servings
Preparation Time: 35 Minutes • Cooking Time: 1¼ Hours

1½	pounds boneless beef round steak, trimmed
2	tablespoons all-purpose flour
	Wesson® No-Stick Cooking Spray
2	large onions, sliced and separated
2	cups peeled, chopped parsnips
1	14½-ounce can Hunt's® Choice-Cut™ Diced Tomatoes with Italian Style Herbs, undrained
1	cup chopped red bell pepper
1	cup water
1½	teaspoons minced fresh basil or ½ teaspoon dried basil, crushed
1	teaspoon reduced-sodium instant beef bouillon granules
½	teaspoon crushed fresh garlic
¼	teaspoon black pepper
1	tablespoon cold water
1	teaspoon cornstarch
2	tablespoons chopped fresh parsley

Cut meat into 6 serving-size pieces. Sprinkle both sides with flour. Using meat mallet, pound flour into meat. Spray unheated no stick skillet with Wesson Cooking Spray; heat over medium heat. Add meat and cook until brown on both sides.

Add onions, parsnips, Hunt's Choice-Cut Tomatoes, bell pepper, the 1 cup water, basil, bouillon granules, garlic, and black pepper. Bring to boil; reduce heat. Simmer, covered, 1¼ hours or until meat and vegetables are tender. Transfer meat and vegetables to serving platter.

Skim fat from tomato mixture. For gravy, stir together the 1 tablespoon water and the cornstarch; add to tomato mixture. Cook and stir until thickened and bubbly. Cook and stir 2 minutes more. Stir in parsley. Serve gravy over meat and vegetables.

Nutrition facts per serving:
257 cal., 30 g pro., 21 g carbo., 6 g total fat (2 g sat. fat), 72 mg chol., 4 g fiber, 480 mg sodium.
Daily Value: 17% vit. A, 80% vit. C, 4% calcium, 21% iron.

OLD-FASHIONED HEARTY BEEF STEW

MAKES 8 SERVINGS
PREPARATION TIME: 25 MINUTES • COOKING TIME: 1 HOUR

- 1½ pounds lean stew beef, trimmed and cut into bite-size pieces
- ⅓ cup all-purpose flour
- ⅓ cup Wesson® Vegetable Oil
- 2 medium onions, cut into 1-inch pieces
- 1 28-ounce can Hunt's® Stewed Tomatoes, undrained
- 1 8-ounce can Hunt's® Tomato Sauce
- 1 cup water*
- 4 medium potatoes, peeled and cubed
- 5 stalks celery, cut into 1-inch pieces
- 6 carrots, peeled and cut into 1-inch pieces
- ½ teaspoon *each:* salt, reduced-sodium instant beef bouillon granules, Italian seasoning, and black pepper
- 1½ tablespoons cornstarch plus 2 tablespoons water, combined

In bag toss beef with flour until well coated. In large Dutch oven heat Wesson Oil. Brown beef with onions until tender. Add *remaining* ingredients *except* cornstarch mixture. Bring to a boil, reduce heat, and simmer, covered, 45 minutes or until beef is tender; stir occasionally.

Gradually stir cornstarch mixture into stew. Continue stirring until sauce thickens. Cover and cook stew an additional 15 minutes, stirring occasionally.

Note: Add a new twist to your stew that everybody will love. Substitute *½ cup* of red wine for *½ cup* of the water and the beef bouillon granules.

NUTRITION FACTS PER SERVING:
400 CAL., 23 G PRO., 36 G CARBO., 19 G TOTAL FAT (5 G SAT. FAT), 63 MG CHOL., 6 G FIBER, 739 MG SODIUM.
DAILY VALUE: 141% VIT. A, 57% VIT. C, 8% CALCIUM, 27% IRON.

CURRIED PORK CHOPS

MAKES 4 SERVINGS
PREPARATION TIME: 20 MINUTES • COOKING TIME: 12 MINUTES

4   pork loin chops, trimmed and cut $^3/_4$ inch thick
    Salt and pepper
    All-purpose flour
2   tablespoons Wesson® Vegetable Oil
$^2/_3$ cup *each:* thinly sliced onion and bell pepper
1   15-ounce can Hunt's® Ready Tomato Sauces
    Chunky Garlic and Herb
1   teaspoon *each:* curry powder and sugar
$^1/_8$ teaspoon cayenne pepper
1   medium apple, cored and thinly sliced
    Hot cooked rice
    Fresh rosemary sprigs for garnish

Sprinkle chops with salt and pepper and coat lightly with flour. In large skillet heat Wesson Oil. Brown chops on both sides; remove.

In drippings sauté onion and bell pepper until vegetables are tender. Stir in Hunt's Ready Sauce, curry powder, sugar, and cayenne pepper. Return chops to skillet, spooning sauce over to coat. Simmer, covered, 10 to 15 minutes or until chops are cooked through. Add apple; heat through. Serve with rice. Garnish with rosemary sprigs.

NUTRITION FACTS PER SERVING:
453 CAL., 25 G PRO., 44 G CARBO., 19 G TOTAL FAT (5 G SAT. FAT), 72 MG CHOL., 3 G FIBER, 418 MG SODIUM.
DAILY VALUE: 5% VIT. A, 67% VIT. C, 10% CALCIUM, 21% IRON.

SAUCY PORK AND TOMATOES

Tomatoes, oregano, and cinnamon give this tasty skillet dish Mediterranean flair. Trim visible fat from 1 pound *boneless pork sirloin;* cut meat into $^1/_2$-inch cubes. In large skillet cook meat, *half* at a time, in 1 tablespoon hot *Wesson® Vegetable Oil* until brown, adding $^1/_2$ of a medium *onion,* cut into wedges, with second portion of meat; drain. Return all meat to skillet. Stir in one 14$^1/_2$-ounce can *Hunts® Choice-Cut™ Diced Tomatoes,* undrained; $^1/_2$ cup *raisins;* $^1/_2$ teaspoon dried *oregano,* crushed; and $^1/_2$ teaspoon ground *cinnamon.* Bring to boil; reduce heat. Simmer, covered, 20 to 25 minutes or until meat is tender. If desired, serve over hot cooked *rice.* Makes 4 servings.

Curried Pork Chops

MEAT

Mediterranean Pork Stew

MAKES 6 SERVINGS
PREPARATION TIME: 30 MINUTES • COOKING TIME: 1 HOUR

1¼	pounds lean boneless pork, trimmed and cut into ¾-inch cubes
1	tablespoon olive oil
½	cup chopped onion
1½	teaspoons crushed fresh garlic
2	cups reduced-sodium, low-fat chicken broth
1	14½-ounce can Hunt's® Whole Tomatoes, undrained and cut up
⅓	cup coarsely chopped roasted red bell pepper*
¼	cup Greek black olives, pitted and cut up
2	teaspoons finely shredded orange peel
1½	teaspoons Italian seasoning
	Dash black pepper
2	medium yellow summer squash, halved lengthwise and sliced
1	11-ounce can mandarin orange sections, drained
3	cups hot cooked couscous or orzo (rosamarina)

In Dutch oven cook meat, *half* at a time, in hot oil until brown. Return all meat to Dutch oven. Add onion and garlic; cook 1 minute. Stir in chicken broth, Hunt's Tomatoes, roasted red pepper, olives, orange peel, Italian seasoning, and black pepper.

Bring to boil; reduce heat. Simmer, covered, 50 minutes. Stir in squash. Simmer, uncovered, 10 minutes more or until meat is tender. Stir in mandarin oranges. Serve with couscous.

Note: To save time, use part of a jar of roasted red bell peppers. You'll find the peppers with the condiments in your supermarket.

NUTRITION FACTS PER SERVING:
300 CAL., 19 G PRO., 34 G CARBO., 10 G TOTAL FAT (3 G SAT. FAT), 43 MG CHOL., 6 G FIBER, 339 MG SODIUM.
DAILY VALUE: 10% VIT. A, 46% VIT. C, 4% CALCIUM, 11% IRON.

CUT UP TOMATOES WITH EASE

It takes just seconds to cut up Hunts® Whole Tomatoes if you leave them right in the can and snip them into pieces with kitchen scissors—oh-so-easy and no bowl to wash!

Italian Veal Stew With Polenta

Makes 4 Servings
Preparation Time: 30 Minutes • Cooking Time: 15 Minutes

	Wesson® No-Stick Cooking Spray
3/4	**cup *each*: coarsely chopped green bell pepper and onion wedges**
1	**teaspoon crushed fresh garlic**
1	**14½-ounce can Hunt's® Choice-Cut™ Diced Tomatoes with Italian Style Herbs, undrained**
1/4	**cup dry red wine**
1	**teaspoon reduced-sodium instant chicken bouillon granules**
1/2	**teaspoon Italian seasoning**
3/4	**pound boneless veal round steak, trimmed and cut ½ inch thick**
2¾	**cups water**
1/8	**teaspoon salt**
3/4	**cup instant polenta**
2	**cups torn fresh spinach**
	Fresh parsley sprigs for garnish

Spray unheated saucepan with Wesson Cooking Spray; heat over medium heat. Add bell pepper, onion, and garlic; cook 4 to 5 minutes or until crisp-tender. Add Hunt's Choice-Cut Tomatoes, wine, bouillon granules, and Italian seasoning. Bring to boil; reduce heat. Simmer, covered, 10 minutes.

Meanwhile, cut meat into bite-size strips. Spray unheated no stick skillet with cooking spray; heat over medium heat. Add meat and cook, stirring constantly, 4 minutes or until no longer pink.

In saucepan bring water and salt to boil. Stir in polenta. Cook, stirring frequently, 5 minutes. Stir meat and spinach into the hot tomato mixture; heat through. Serve over polenta. Garnish with parsley sprigs.

NUTRITION FACTS PER SERVING:
349 CAL., 26 G PRO., 50 G CARBO., 4 G TOTAL FAT (1 G SAT. FAT), 69 MG CHOL., 7 G FIBER, 801 MG SODIUM.
DAILY VALUE: 27% VIT. A, 62% VIT. C, 6% CALCIUM, 15% IRON.

MEAT ALTERNATIVES

In a healthful diet, which comes first—the chicken or the egg? Neither! Both are delicious alternatives to red meat in the protein category of the pyramid, along with fish, dry beans, peas, and other legumes. And, when sauced with Hunt's® tomato products, these hearty recipes will stand out as family favorites for years to come.

Recommendation:
2 to 3 servings a day from this and the meat group

Blackened Chicken Sa.
(see recipe, page 70)

Blackened Chicken Salad

- $1/4$ cup *each:* fresh lemon juice and country-style Dijon mustard
- 2 tablespoons Wesson® Vegetable Oil
- 2 $14^1/2$-ounce cans Hunt's® Choice-Cut™ Diced Tomatoes with Roasted Garlic, drained
- $3/4$ cup diced yellow bell pepper
- $1/4$ cup finely chopped red onion
- 3 tablespoons cider vinegar
- 1 tablespoon sugar
- 4 boneless, skinless chicken breast halves, slightly pounded
- 1 to 3 tablespoons Cajun seasoning Wesson® No-Stick Cooking Spray
- $3/4$ to 1 pound snap peas
- 8 cups torn mixed greens
- $1/2$ cup *each:* yellow or orange bell pepper, cut into strips, and sliced cucumber

In blender or food processor blend lemon juice, mustard, and Wesson Oil on high speed 30 seconds. Pour dressing into small bowl; cover and refrigerate. In another bowl mix Hunt's Choice-Cut Tomatoes and *next 4* ingredients, ending with sugar, until well blended. Cover and refrigerate relish.

Generously rub chicken with Cajun seasoning. Heavily coat large unheated skillet with Wesson Cooking Spray. Over medium heat pan-fry chicken 5 to 7 minutes on *each* side; cook until juices run clear. Remove chicken from skillet; let cool. Meanwhile, steam peas 2 minutes. Rinse in cold water until peas are completely cool; drain.

In large bowl combine peas, greens, bell pepper, and cucumber; toss vegetables with dressing until well coated. Evenly divide salad mixture onto 4 plates. Top *each* salad with *$1/2$ cup* relish. Place *1* sliced chicken breast half over *each* salad; top with additional relish.

NUTRITION FACTS PER SERVING:
342 CAL., 29 G PRO., 31 G CARBO., 12 G TOTAL FAT (2 G SAT. FAT), 59 MG CHOL., 6 G FIBER, 1,450 MG SODIUM.
DAILY VALUE: 57% VIT. A, 208% VIT. C, 15% CALCIUM, 25% IRON.

No-Prep Chicken and Rice

Makes 6 Servings
Preparation Time: 10 Minutes • Cooking Time: 1 Hour
Standing Time: 5 Minutes

	Wesson® No-Stick Cooking Spray
1	**cup brown rice**
2	**pounds boneless skinless chicken tenders, rinsed and patted dry**
2	**14½-ounce cans Hunt's® Choice-Cut™ Diced Tomatoes with Crushed Red Pepper and Basil, undrained**
1	**15½-ounce can small red beans, drained**
2	**7-ounce cans whole kernel corn with red and green peppers, drained**
½	**cup reduced-sodium, low-fat chicken broth**
1	**4-ounce can diced green chiles**
½	**teaspoon garlic salt**
	Chopped fresh cilantro for garnish

Generously spray 13x9x2-inch baking dish with Wesson Cooking Spray. Preheat oven to 350°. Evenly spread rice in baking dish; place chicken tenders over rice.

Pour *remaining* ingredients *except* cilantro over chicken; lightly mix vegetables. Bake, covered, 1 to 1¼ hours or until rice is tender. Halfway through baking, stir juices with rice. Let stand 5 minutes before serving. Garnish with cilantro.

Nutrition Facts per Serving:
339 cal., 38 g pro., 39 g carbo., 6 g total fat (1 g sat. fat), 79 mg chol., 7 g fiber, 819 mg sodium.
Daily Value: 12% vit. A, 53% vit. C, 7% calcium, 17% iron.

CHUNKY CITRUS CHICKEN

Accent a 15-ounce can of *Hunts® Ready Tomato Sauces Chunky Special* with a little finely shredded *orange peel*, a splash of fresh *orange juice*, and a dash of *ground red pepper*. This delightful sauce is great to serve with broiled or sautéed chicken breasts and hot cooked pasta. Top with grated Parmesan or Romano cheese.

CHEESE-STUFFED CHICKEN ROLLS

MAKES 4 SERVINGS
PREPARATION TIME: 30 MINUTES • COOKING TIME: 37 MINUTES

1/3	cup diced sweet onion
2	tablespoons *each:* chopped fresh parsley and grated reduced-fat Parmesan cheese
1/4	teaspoon *each:* pepper, garlic powder, and paprika
4	3/4-ounce slices reduced-fat Swiss cheese
4	boneless, skinless chicken breast halves, pounded to 1/8-inch thickness
1/2	cup seasoned dry bread crumbs
2	tablespoons grated reduced-fat Parmesan cheese
1/3	cup all-purpose flour
2	eggs, lightly beaten*
2	tablespoons Wesson® Vegetable Oil
2	15-ounce cans Hunt's® Ready Tomato Sauces Chunky Special
	Hot cooked brown rice (optional)

In small bowl combine *first 6* ingredients, ending with paprika; mix well and set aside. Place one slice of cheese in center of *each* breast half. Top with *1/4* of the onion mixture. Starting with long edge, tightly roll breast half, folding in ends to seal the cheese and onion mixture. Fasten seam sides with toothpicks.

In small bowl combine bread crumbs and Parmesan cheese. Dredge *each* roll in flour. Dip *each* stuffed breast half into eggs, then roll in bread crumb mixture.

In large skillet heat Wesson Oil over medium flame. Fry chicken, starting with seam side down, 7 to 10 minutes, rotating to avoid overbrowning. Cover and continue to fry an additional 20 minutes. Remove skillet from heat. Remove chicken rolls from skillet. Gently remove toothpicks from rolls.

Add Hunt's Ready Sauce to skillet; top with chicken rolls. Cook, covered, for an additional 10 minutes or until juices from chicken run clear. Before serving, spoon sauce over rolls. Serve over rice, if desired.

Note: If you're watching your fat and cholesterol closely, substitute 1/2 cup refrigerated or frozen egg product, thawed, for the 2 eggs.

NUTRITION FACTS PER SERVING:
521 CAL., 36 G PRO., 52 G CARBO., 19 G TOTAL FAT (4 G SAT. FAT), 177 MG CHOL., 4 G FIBER, 1,762 MG SODIUM.
DAILY VALUE: 48% VIT. A, 58% VIT. C, 13% CALCIUM, 12% IRON.

MEAT ALTERNATIVES

Cheese-Stuffed Chicken Rolls

Quick-and-Easy Chicken Parmesan

MAKES 6 SERVINGS
TOTAL TIME: 25 MINUTES

1	12-ounce box linguine
2	tablespoons Wesson® Oil
½	cup *each:* diced onion and diced bell pepper
1	14½-ounce can Hunt's® Choice-Cut™ Diced Tomatoes, undrained
1	15-ounce can Hunt's® Ready Tomato Sauces Original Italian
1	4-ounce can sliced mushrooms, drained
1	teaspoon sugar
½	teaspoon *each:* garlic salt and Italian seasoning
1	13½-ounce box breaded chicken patties
3	slices provolone cheese, cut in half
	Grated reduced-fat Parmesan cheese for garnish
	Chopped fresh parsley for garnish

Preheat oven to 425°. Cook linguine according to package directions.

Meanwhile, in saucepan in hot Wesson Oil, sauté onion and pepper until crisp-tender. Add Hunt's Diced Tomatoes, Hunt's Ready Sauce, and *next 4* ingredients, ending with Italian seasoning; blend well. Cover, simmer 10 minutes, stirring occasionally.

While sauce and pasta are cooking, line baking sheet with foil. Place chicken patties on baking sheet. Bake chicken 10 to 12 minutes. Spoon about *2 tablespoons* of sauce over chicken and top with provolone cheese. Bake 1 to 2 minutes or until cheese is lightly melted.

Toss pasta with *half* of the *remaining* pasta sauce. Place tossed pasta on serving platter. Top with *remaining* sauce and chicken patties. Garnish with Parmesan cheese and parsley.

NUTRITION FACTS PER SERVING:
544 CAL., 29 G PRO., 64 G CARBO., 20 G TOTAL FAT (4 G SAT. FAT), 72 MG CHOL., 3 G FIBER, 1,442 MG SODIUM. DAILY VALUE: 21% VIT. A, 37% VIT. C, 17% CALCIUM, 26% IRON.

Santa Fe Chicken and Dumplings

Makes 6 Servings
Preparation Time: 10 Minutes • Cooking Time: 18 Minutes

2	cups cooked, diced chicken
2	14$^{1}/_{2}$-ounce cans Hunt's® Choice-Cut™ Diced Tomatoes, undrained
1	15-ounce can spicy chili beans, undrained
1	cup frozen whole kernel corn, thawed
1$^{1}/_{2}$	cups reduced-fat all-purpose baking mix
$^{1}/_{2}$	cup cornmeal
$^{2}/_{3}$	cup skim milk
$^{1}/_{4}$	cup sliced green onions
$^{1}/_{2}$	cup shredded reduced-fat cheddar cheese

In Dutch oven combine chicken and Hunt's Choice-Cut Tomatoes. Bring to a boil and reduce heat to low. Cover and simmer 5 minutes, stirring occasionally. Stir in beans and corn.

Meanwhile, in medium bowl combine *remaining* ingredients *except* cheese. Mix until a soft dough forms. Drop by 12 rounded spoonfuls onto hot chili. Cook, uncovered, 10 minutes. Sprinkle with cheese. Cover and cook an additional 3 minutes or until cheese has melted.

Nutrition facts per serving:
418 cal., 27 g pro., 50 g carbo., 12 g total fat (4 g sat. fat), 64 mg chol., 4 g fiber, 1,159 mg sodium.
Daily Value: 16% vit. A, 40% vit. C, 17% calcium, 36% iron.

COOKED CHICKEN IN MINUTES

There's no need to roast a whole chicken to make Santa Fe Chicken and Dumplings (see recipe, above). You can quickly poach some chicken breasts instead. Just place 12 ounces *skinless, boneless chicken breasts* in a skillet with 1 cup *water*. Bring to boil; reduce heat. Simmer, covered, 12 to 14 minutes or until chicken is tender and no longer pink. Drain and chop the chicken.

Down-Home Chicken and Sausage Jambalaya

MAKES 6 SERVINGS
PREPARATION TIME: 20 MINUTES • COOKING TIME: 8 MINUTES

2	tablespoons Wesson® Vegetable Oil
1/2	pound chicken tenders, cut into 1-inch pieces
1	teaspoon crushed fresh garlic
1/2	pound "lite" smoked Polish sausage, cut into 1/4-inch slices
1	cup diced onion
3/4	cup chopped green bell pepper
1	14 1/2-ounce can Hunt's® Choice-Cut™ Diced Tomatoes with Roasted Garlic, undrained
1/2	cup reduced-sodium, low-fat chicken broth
1/4	cup chopped fresh parsley
1/2	teaspoon *each:* dried thyme, crushed, and salt
1/4	teaspoon *each:* black pepper and ground red pepper
1	tablespoon cornstarch plus 2 tablespoons water
4	cups hot cooked rice

In large skillet heat Wesson Oil until hot. Stir-fry chicken and garlic until chicken is browned. Add sausage and stir-fry an additional 4 to 5 minutes. Remove from skillet to medium bowl; cover and set aside.

In same skillet sauté onion and bell pepper until tender. Add sausage, chicken, and *remaining* ingredients *except* rice. Bring to a boil. Reduce heat and simmer, uncovered, 8 to 10 minutes. Serve over hot cooked rice.

NUTRITION FACTS PER SERVING:
312 CAL., 17 G PRO., 38 G CARBO., 8 G TOTAL FAT (1 G SAT. FAT), 43 MG CHOL., 1 G FIBER, 858 MG SODIUM.
DAILY VALUE: 7% VIT. A, 54% VIT. C, 5% CALCIUM, 15% IRON.

Harvest Chicken and Sweet Potato Stew

MAKES 4 SERVINGS
PREPARATION TIME: 15 MINUTES • COOKING TIME: 25 MINUTES

4	boneless, skinless chicken breast halves
	Garlic salt and pepper
1/2	cup all-purpose flour
2	tablespoons Wesson® Vegetable Oil
2	cups cubed, peeled sweet potatoes*
1	cup chopped onion
1	14 1/2-ounce can Hunt's® Stewed Tomatoes, undrained and crushed lightly
3/4	cup each: reduced-sodium, low-fat chicken broth and apple cider
1/2	teaspoon dried dillweed
	Dash hot pepper sauce

Rinse and pat dry chicken. Cut chicken into 1/2-inch pieces. Sprinkle with garlic salt and pepper. Place flour in plastic bag. Add chicken; shake until chicken is well coated.

In large stockpot heat Wesson Oil and brown chicken on both sides until golden brown. Remove chicken and set aside.

Add sweet potatoes and onion; sauté until onion is tender. Stir in *remaining* ingredients; blend well. Add browned chicken and bring to a boil. Reduce heat, cover, and simmer 25 to 30 minutes or until chicken is cooked and potatoes are tender; stir often.

*Note: Yams can be substituted for a sweeter stew.

NUTRITION FACTS PER SERVING:
365 CAL., 26 G PRO., 42 G CARBO., 10 G TOTAL FAT (2 G SAT. FAT), 60 MG CHOL., 5 G FIBER, 452 MG SODIUM.
DAILY VALUE: 140% VIT. A, 65% VIT. C, 6% CALCIUM, 17% IRON.

Southwest Turkey Chili Soup

MAKES 8 SERVINGS
PREPARATION TIME: 15 MINUTES • COOKING TIME: 20 MINUTES

	Wesson® No-Stick Cooking Spray
1/2	pound ground turkey
4	cups reduced-sodium, low-fat chicken broth
1	15¼-ounce can reduced-sodium, dark red kidney beans, rinsed and drained
1	15-ounce can Hunt's® Ready Tomato Sauces Chunky Chili
1	8-ounce can Hunt's® Tomato Sauce
1	7-ounce can whole kernel corn with red and green peppers, drained
1	teaspoon chili powder
1/2	teaspoon ground cumin
	Shredded reduced-fat sharp cheddar cheese for garnish
	Crushed baked tortilla chips for garnish

Lightly spray large unheated saucepan with Wesson Cooking Spray. Add ground turkey and cook until brown. Add *remaining* ingredients *except* cheese and tortilla chips; mix well.

Cover and bring to a boil. Reduce heat and simmer 20 to 25 minutes, stirring occasionally. Serve immediately. Garnish with cheese and chips.

NUTRITION FACTS PER SERVING:
134 CAL., 9 G PRO., 20 G CARBO., 3 G TOTAL FAT (1 G SAT. FAT), 11 MG CHOL., 3 G FIBER, 954 MG SODIUM.
DAILY VALUE: 4% VIT. A, 14% VIT. C, 5% CALCIUM, 11% IRON.

LET'S TALK TURKEY

When it comes to fat and calories, not all ground turkey is the same. Some contains turkey skin, which adds both fat and calories. The most healthful choice is to select a brand that contains no skin. If it's not available, ask your butcher to grind fresh turkey breast for you.

CREOLE SHRIMP AND RICE

MAKES 6 TO 8 SERVINGS
PREPARATION TIME: 15 MINUTES • COOKING TIME: 30 MINUTES

1	pound medium-size shrimp, shelled with tails left on, deveined, and rinsed
1	tablespoon Wesson® Canola Oil
1	cup *each:* diced onion, chopped green and/or yellow bell pepper
2	teaspoons crushed fresh garlic
6	ounces pepperoni, cut into $1/4$-inch-thick slices
1	28-ounce can Hunt's® Stewed Tomatoes, undrained
$1^{1}/2$	cups converted rice
1	cup water
2	to 3 teaspoons Creole seasoning
1	10-ounce package frozen whole okra, cut in half and thawed

Rinse and pat dry shrimp; set aside. In large Dutch oven heat Wesson Oil until hot. Sauté onion, pepper, and garlic until crisp-tender. Add pepperoni and cook an additional 3 minutes. Stir in Hunt's Tomatoes, rice, water, and Creole seasoning. Bring to a boil. Reduce heat, cover, and simmer 20 minutes, stirring occasionally. Stir in shrimp and okra. Cover and cook an additional 10 minutes or until rice is tender, stirring occasionally.

NUTRITION FACTS PER SERVING:
447 CAL., 22 G PRO., 56 G CARBO., 16 G TOTAL FAT (5 G SAT. FAT), 123 MG CHOL., 3 G FIBER, 1,082 MG SODIUM.
DAILY VALUE: 18% VIT. A, 89% VIT. C, 10% CALCIUM, 35% IRON.

HAM JAMBALAYA

With the help of Hunt's® Ready Sauces, you can take a culinary trip to Cajun country anytime you like by making this four-ingredient jambalaya. In a medium skillet heat one 15-ounce can *Hunt's® Ready Tomato Sauces Chunky Special,* 1 cup uncooked *long grain rice,* and $1/2$ cup *water.* When the mixture boils, stir in some cubed *fully cooked turkey ham* and enough *chili powder* to suit your taste. Reduce the heat. Simmer, covered, about 20 minutes or until the liquid is absorbed. Stir before serving to fluff the rice.

Fish Veracruz

MAKES 4 SERVINGS
PREPARATION TIME: 15 MINUTES • COOKING TIME: 8 MINUTES

1   pound fresh or frozen skinless cod, red snapper,
      or orange roughy fillets
    Wesson® No-Stick Cooking Spray
1   medium onion, sliced and separated into rings
1/2 teaspoon crushed fresh garlic
1   14 1/2-ounce can Hunt's® Choice-Cut™ Diced
      Tomatoes, undrained
1/4 cup *each:* sliced pimiento-stuffed green olives and
      dry white wine
1   to 2 fresh or canned jalapeño peppers, seeded
      and chopped (1 tablespoon) (see tip, page 42)
1   bay leaf
1/2 teaspoon sugar
    Dash ground cinnamon
1   cup water
3   cups hot cooked spinach linguine

Thaw fish, if frozen. Cut fish into 4 serving-size pieces. Measure thickness of fish. Spray unheated saucepan with Wesson Cooking Spray. Add onion and garlic and cook until onion is tender.

Stir in Hunt's Choice-Cut Tomatoes, olives, wine, jalapeño peppers, bay leaf, sugar, and cinnamon. Bring to boil; reduce heat. Simmer, uncovered, 8 to 10 minutes or until slightly thickened. Discard bay leaf.

Meanwhile, in skillet bring water to boil; add fish. Return to boil; reduce heat. Simmer, covered, until fish flakes easily with fork. Allow 4 to 6 minutes per 1/2-inch thickness of fish. Serve fish over linguine. Spoon tomato mixture over fish and linguine.

NUTRITION FACTS PER SERVING:
286 CAL., 23 G PRO., 41 G CARBO., 3 G TOTAL FAT (0 G SAT. FAT), 43 MG CHOL., 1 G FIBER, 467 MG SODIUM.
DAILY VALUE: 7% VIT. A, 38% VIT. C, 5% CALCIUM, 18% IRON.

MEAT ALTERNATIVES

Fish Veracruz

Baked Fish Fillets With Herbed Tomato Sauce

MAKES 6 SERVINGS
PREPARATION TIME: 20 MINUTES • COOKING TIME: 7 MINUTES

1½	pounds fresh or frozen skinless haddock, orange roughy, or cod fillets, thawed
	Wesson® No-Stick Cooking Spray
½	teaspoon lemon-pepper seasoning
2	cups sliced fresh mushrooms
1	cup chopped green bell pepper
½	cup chopped onion
¼	cup water
1	15-ounce can Hunt's® Ready Tomato Sauces Chunky Special
1½	teaspoons chopped fresh oregano or ½ teaspoon dried oregano, crushed
½	cup shredded reduced-fat mozzarella cheese
3	cups hot cooked spinach fettuccine

Cut fish into 6 serving-size pieces. Measure thickness of fish. Spray 2-quart rectangular baking dish with Wesson Cooking Spray. Place fish in dish, tucking under any thin portions. Sprinkle with lemon-pepper seasoning.

Bake in 450° oven until fish flakes easily with fork. Allow 6 to 9 minutes per ½-inch thickness of fish. Drain off any liquid.

Meanwhile, for sauce, in covered saucepan cook mushrooms, bell pepper, and onion in water 5 minutes or until vegetables are tender; drain. Stir in Hunt's Ready Sauce and oregano. Heat through.

Spoon sauce over fish; sprinkle with cheese. Bake 1 minute more or until cheese melts. Serve with fettuccine.

NUTRITION FACTS PER SERVING:
231 CAL., 25 G PRO., 25 G CARBO., 3 G TOTAL FAT (1 G SAT. FAT), 49 MG CHOL., 2 G FIBER, 664 MG SODIUM.
DAILY VALUE: 10% VIT. A, 41% VIT. C, 9% CALCIUM, 11% IRON.

Huevos Rancheros

MAKES 6 SERVINGS
PREPARATION TIME: 25 MINUTES • COOKING TIME: 28 MINUTES

2	tablespoons Wesson® Vegetable Oil
1	cup *each:* diced onion, diced red and/or green bell pepper
1	teaspoon crushed fresh garlic
1	15-ounce can Hunt's® Ready Tomato Sauces Chunky Special
1	14½-ounce can Hunt's® Whole Tomatoes, drained and chopped
1	tablespoon chopped fresh cilantro
½	tablespoon diced fresh jalapeño peppers, seeds removed (optional) (see tip, page 42)
1	teaspoon sugar
¼	teaspoon salt
⅛	teaspoon black pepper
6	large eggs
⅓	cup Wesson® Vegetable Oil
6	corn tortillas
	Cilantro sprigs for garnish

In large skillet heat 2 tablespoons Wesson Oil until hot. Sauté onion, bell pepper, and garlic until onion is tender. Add Hunt's Ready Sauce, Hunt's Tomatoes, and *next* 5 ingredients, ending with black pepper. Simmer, uncovered, 20 minutes, stirring occasionally.

Using wooden spoon, make an indentation in sauce; crack an egg into indentation. Repeat with *remaining* eggs.

Cover and cook eggs over low heat 10 to 14 minutes or until desired doneness.

Meanwhile, in another skillet heat ⅓ cup Wesson Oil until hot. Fry tortillas, 10 seconds on *each* side. Remove and drain on paper towels. Overlap tortillas on large serving platter. Gently slide eggs with sauce from skillet onto fried tortillas. Garnish with cilantro sprigs.

NUTRITION FACTS PER SERVING:
265 CAL., 10 G PRO., 24 G CARBO., 15 G TOTAL FAT (3 G SAT. FAT), 213 MG CHOL., 2 G FIBER, 762 MG SODIUM.
DAILY VALUE: 33% VIT. A, 106% VIT. C, 9% CALCIUM, 11% IRON.

Farmer's Breakfast

MAKES 6 SERVINGS
PREPARATION TIME: 15 MINUTES • COOKING TIME: 20 MINUTES

2	tablespoons Wesson® Best Blend Oil
3	cups frozen, shredded hash brown potatoes, thawed
3/4	cup sliced green onions
1	14½-ounce can Hunt's® Choice-Cut™ Diced Tomatoes with Roasted Garlic, drained
1½	cups fat-free, large seasoned croutons
6	large eggs, beaten
3/4	cup diced reduced-fat, reduced-sodium ham
2/3	cup shredded reduced-fat cheddar cheese
1/8	to ¼ teaspoon coarse ground pepper (optional)

In 12-inch skillet heat Wesson Oil; add hash browns and *½ cup* green onions. Fry until potatoes are deep golden brown; stir occasionally. Add more oil if potatoes become dry.

Add Hunt's Choice-Cut Tomatoes and *remaining* ingredients *except* remaining green onions; blend well. Cook egg mixture until eggs are set. Salt to taste. Garnish with *remaining* green onions.

NUTRITION FACTS PER SERVING:
299 CAL., 17 G PRO., 28 G CARBO., 13 G TOTAL FAT (4 G SAT. FAT), 230 MG CHOL., 3 G FIBER, 914 MG SODIUM.
DAILY VALUE: 18% VIT. A, 44% VIT. C, 12% CALCIUM, 16% IRON.

MEAT ALTERNATIVES

Farmer's Breakfast

ZESTY DEVILED EGGS

MAKES 20 APPETIZER SERVINGS
TOTAL TIME: 30 MINUTES

10	hard-boiled extra large eggs, peeled and halved
1/3	cup reduced-fat mayonnaise
1	teaspoon Dijon mustard
1/4	cup Hunt's® Choice-Cut™ Diced Tomatoes with Roasted Garlic (see tip below)
3	tablespoons thinly sliced green onion
2	tablespoons finely chopped pitted black olives
1	tablespoon finely chopped pickled jalapeño peppers
1/4	teaspoon salt

Remove yolks from eggs and place in medium bowl. Add mayonnaise and mustard; blend well. Add *remaining* ingredients; mix thoroughly. Evenly spoon mixture into egg white halves.

NUTRITION FACTS PER SERVING:
54 CAL., 3 G PRO., 1 G CARBO., 4 G TOTAL FAT (1 G SAT. FAT), 107 MG CHOL., 0 G FIBER, 115 MG SODIUM.
DAILY VALUE: 4% VIT. A, 1% VIT. C, 1% CALCIUM, 2% IRON.

THE TREASURE IN THE FREEZER

Having some leftover Hunt's® Choice-Cut™ Diced Tomatoes with Roasted Garlic is never a problem. Seal the tomatoes in a freezer bag and freeze for up to 3 months. Then, thaw and use them to add a rich garlic-and-tomato flavor to soup, stew, or chili. Or, heat the tomatoes with other vegetables as a side dish, toss them into pasta salad, or use to make salsa.

Spicy Corn Chili

MAKES 4 SERVINGS
PREPARATION TIME: 20 MINUTES • COOKING TIME: 20 MINUTES

- $1/2$ **cup chopped onion**
- 1 **tablespoon Wesson® Oil**
- 1 **teaspoon dried oregano, crushed**
- $3/4$ **teaspoon ground cumin**
- 1 **$14^{1}/_{2}$-ounce can Hunt's® Choice-Cut™ Diced Tomatoes with Roasted Garlic**
- 1 **8-ounce can Hunt's® Tomato Sauce**
- $1/2$ **cup beer**
- 1 **15-ounce can black beans, rinsed and drained**
- 1 **cup frozen whole kernel corn**
- $1/4$ **cup chopped canned jalapeño peppers**
- $1/8$ **teaspoon black pepper**
  Hot cooked rice (optional)

Cook onion in hot Wesson Oil until tender. Stir in oregano and cumin; cook and stir 1 minute. Drain Hunt's Choice-Cut Tomatoes, reserving juice. Set aside. Add reserved juice, Hunt's Tomato Sauce, and beer to skillet. Simmer, uncovered, 5 minutes. Stir in reserved tomatoes, beans, corn, jalapeño peppers, and black pepper. Simmer, uncovered, 15 to 20 minutes. If desired, serve over rice.

NUTRITION FACTS PER SERVING:
191 CAL., 10 G PRO., 33 G CARBO., 4 G TOTAL FAT (1 G SAT. FAT), 0 MG CHOL., 7 G FIBER, 1,050 MG SODIUM.
DAILY VALUE: 14% VIT. A, 71% VIT. C, 7% CALCIUM, 18% IRON.

Black-Eyed Peas and Rice

MAKES 4 SERVINGS
PREPARATION TIME: 20 MINUTES • COOKING TIME: 15 MINUTES

- $2/3$ **cup vegetable broth**
- $1/3$ **cup chopped onion**
- $1/2$ **cup quick-cooking brown rice**
- 1 **tablespoon chopped celery tops**
- 1 **15-ounce can black-eyed peas, rinsed and drained**
- 1 **$14^{1}/_{2}$-ounce can Hunt's® Choice-Cut™ Diced Tomatoes with Roasted Garlic, undrained**

In saucepan combine $1/3$ *cup* of the broth and onion. Simmer, covered, 2 minutes or until onion is tender. Stir in rice, *remaining* $1/3$ cup broth, and celery. Simmer, covered, 10 minutes or just until rice is tender. Stir in black-eyed peas and Hunt's Choice-Cut Tomatoes. Cook, uncovered, 5 to 8 minutes more or until desired consistency.

NUTRITION FACTS PER SERVING:
160 CAL., 8 G PRO., 31 G CARBO., 1 G TOTAL FAT (0 G SAT. FAT), 0 MG CHOL., 6 G FIBER, 892 MG SODIUM.
DAILY VALUE: 8% VIT. A, 27% VIT. C, 4% CALCIUM, 3% IRON.

TRIPLE BEAN COMBO

MAKES 8 SERVINGS
PREPARATION TIME: 25 MINUTES • COOKING TIME: 15 MINUTES

1	15$^1\!/_2$-ounce can garbanzo beans, rinsed and drained
1	15$^1\!/_4$-ounce can *each:* kidney beans and green lima beans, rinsed and drained
1	14$^1\!/_2$-ounce can Hunt's® Choice-Cut™ Diced Tomatoes with Italian Style Herbs, undrained
$^2\!/_3$	cup *each:* chopped red and yellow bell pepper
$^1\!/_4$	cup *each:* diced red onion and chopped fresh parsley
1	teaspoon crushed fresh garlic
$^1\!/_2$	teaspoon salt
$^1\!/_4$	teaspoon coarse ground pepper
	Fresh cilantro sprigs for garnish
	Toasted tortilla wedges for garnish

In medium-size saucepan combine *all* ingredients *except* cilantro sprigs; mix well. Bring mixture to boil, stirring occasionally. Reduce heat. Cover and simmer 15 minutes or until vegetables are tender, stirring occasionally. Garnish with cilantro sprigs and tortilla wedges.

NUTRITION FACTS PER SERVING:
127 CAL., 8 G PRO., 25 G CARBO., 1 G TOTAL FAT (0 G SAT. FAT), 0 MG CHOL., 5 G FIBER, 750 MG SODIUM.
DAILY VALUE: 11% VIT. A, 72% VIT. C, 4% CALCIUM, 16% IRON.

START WITH A BAKED POTATO

A baked potato becomes a whole meal if you spoon on this easy chicken-and-tomato topper. In a saucepan stir together one 15-ounce can *Hunt's® Ready Tomato Sauces Chunky Special;* 1 cup cubed *cooked chicken;* 1 cup *frozen whole kernel corn;* $^1\!/_4$ cup thinly sliced *green onions;* $^1\!/_2$ teaspoon dried *rosemary* or *thyme,* crushed; and $^1\!/_4$ teaspoon *pepper.* Cook and stir until heated through. Spoon over 4 *baked potatoes.* Sprinkle with $^1\!/_2$ cup shredded *reduced-fat Colby-Monterey Jack cheese.* Makes 4 servings.

LENTIL AND TOMATO STEW

MAKES 4 SIDE-DISH SERVINGS
PREPARATION TIME: 25 MINUTES • COOKING TIME: 35 MINUTES

¹/₂	cup chopped onion
1	teaspoon crushed fresh garlic
1	tablespoon Wesson® Oil
4	cups water
1	cup dry lentils, rinsed and drained
1	7¹/₂-ounce can Hunt's® Whole Tomatoes, undrained and cut up
1	tablespoon Worcestershire sauce
2	teaspoons instant vegetable or reduced-sodium chicken bouillon granules
1	bay leaf
1¹/₂	teaspoons chopped fresh thyme or ¹/₂ teaspoon dried thyme, crushed
¹/₄	teaspoon *each:* fennel seed, crushed, and pepper
1	10-ounce package frozen chopped spinach
1	cup chopped carrots
1	tablespoon balsamic or red wine vinegar

In Dutch oven cook onion and garlic in hot Wesson Oil until onion is tender. Stir in water, lentils, Hunt's Tomatoes, Worcestershire sauce, bouillon granules, bay leaf, thyme, fennel seed, and pepper. Bring to boil; reduce heat. Simmer, covered, 20 minutes, stirring the mixture occasionally.

Add frozen spinach and carrots. Return to boil, breaking up spinach. Reduce heat. Simmer, covered, 15 minutes more or until lentils are tender. Stir in vinegar. Discard bay leaf.

NUTRITION FACTS PER SERVING:
119 CAL., 6 G PRO., 19 G CARBO., 4 G TOTAL FAT (1 G SAT. FAT), 0 MG CHOL., 5 G FIBER, 640 MG SODIUM.
DAILY VALUE: 159% VIT. A, 54% VIT. C, 12% CALCIUM, 19% IRON.

MEAT ALTERNATIVES

RECIPE INDEX

TIPS

NUTRITION FIGURES

Each recipe in this book lists the nutrition facts for one serving. Here's how these values were calculated. When a recipe gives a choice of ingredients (such as black-eyed peas or black beans), the first choice was used for the analysis. If an ingredient is listed as optional in a recipe, it was not included in the analysis. All values were rounded to the nearest whole number.

RECIPE CATEGORY INDEX

RECIPES-BY-PRODUCT INDEX

Metric Cooking Hints

By making a few conversions, cooks in Australia, Canada, and the United Kingdom can use these recipes with confidence. The charts on this page provide a guide for converting measurements from the U.S. customary system, which is used through-out this book, to the imperial and metric systems. There also is a conversion table for oven temperatures to accommodate the differences in oven calibrations.

Product Differences: Most of the ingredients called for in the recipes in this book are available in English-speaking countries. However, some are known by different names. Here are some common American ingredients and their possible counterparts:
■ Sugar is granulated or castor sugar.
■ Powdered sugar is icing sugar.
■ All-purpose flour is plain household flour or white flour. When self-rising flour is used in place of all-purpose flour in a recipe that calls for leavening, omit the leavening agent (baking soda or baking powder) and salt.
■ Light corn syrup is golden syrup.
■ Cornstarch is cornflour.
■ Baking soda is bicarbonate of soda.
■ Vanilla is vanilla essence.
■ Green, red, or yellow bell peppers are capsicums.
■ Golden raisins are sultanas.

Volume and Weight: Americans traditionally use cup measures for liquid and solid ingredients. The chart, top right, shows the approximate imperial and metric equivalents. If you are accustomed to weighing solid ingredients, the following approximate equivalents will be helpful.
■ 1 cup butter, castor sugar, or rice = 8 ounces = about 250 grams
■ 1 cup flour = 4 ounces = about 125 grams
■ 1 cup icing sugar = 5 ounces = about 150 grams
　Spoon measures are used for smaller amounts of ingredients. Although the size of the tablespoon varies slightly in different countries, for practical purposes and for recipes in this book, a straight substitution is all that's necessary.
　Measurements made using cups or spoons always should be level unless stated otherwise.

Equivalents: U.S. = Australia/U.K.

$\frac{1}{8}$ teaspoon = 0.5 ml
$\frac{1}{4}$ teaspoon = 1 ml
$\frac{1}{2}$ teaspoon = 2 ml
1 teaspoon = 5 ml
1 tablespoon = 1 tablespoon
$\frac{1}{4}$ cup = 2 tablespoons = 2 fluid ounces = 60 ml
$\frac{1}{3}$ cup = $\frac{1}{4}$ cup = 3 fluid ounces = 90 ml
$\frac{1}{2}$ cup = $\frac{1}{3}$ cup = 4 fluid ounces = 120 ml
$\frac{2}{3}$ cup = $\frac{1}{2}$ cup = 5 fluid ounces = 150 ml
$\frac{3}{4}$ cup = $\frac{2}{3}$ cup = 6 fluid ounces = 180 ml
1 cup = $\frac{3}{4}$ cup = 8 fluid ounces = 240 ml
$1\frac{1}{4}$ cups = 1 cup
2 cups = 1 pint
1 quart = 1 liter
$\frac{1}{2}$ inch = 1.27 cm
1 inch = 2.54 cm

Baking Pan Sizes

American	Metric
8×1½-inch round baking pan	20×4-cm cake tin
9×1½-inch round baking pan	23×3.5-cm cake tin
11×7×1½-inch baking pan	28×18×4-cm baking tin
13×9×2-inch baking pan	30×20×3-cm baking tin
2-quart rectangular baking dish	30×20×3-cm baking tin
15×10×1-inch baking pan	30×25×2-cm baking tin (Swiss roll tin)
9-inch pie plate	22×4- or 23×4-cm pie plate
7- or 8-inch springform pan	18- or 20-cm springform or loose-bottom cake tin
9×5×3-inch loaf pan	23×13×7-cm or 2-pound narrow loaf tin or pâté tin
1½-quart casserole	1.5-liter casserole
2-quart casserole	2-liter casserole

Oven Temperature Equivalents

Fahrenheit Setting	Celsius Setting*	Gas Setting
300°F	150°C	Gas Mark 2 (slow)
325°F	160°C	Gas Mark 3 (moderately slow)
350°F	180°C	Gas Mark 4 (moderate)
375°F	190°C	Gas Mark 5 (moderately hot)
400°F	200°C	Gas Mark 6 (hot)
425°F	220°C	Gas Mark 7
450°F	230°C	Gas Mark 8 (very hot)
Broil		Grill

*Electric and gas ovens may be calibrated using Celsius. However, for an electric oven, increase the Celsius setting 10 to 20 degrees when cooking above 160°C. For convection or forced-air ovens (gas or electric), lower the temperature setting 10°C when cooking at all heat levels.